The Pianist's Problems

To Cheryl
Surprevant

Warm regards
21 June 68
Wm S Newman

THE

Pianist's Problems

A MODERN APPROACH TO
EFFICIENT PRACTICE AND
MUSICIANLY PERFORMANCE

Revised and Enlarged

By WILLIAM S. NEWMAN, Ph.D.

Professor of Music and
Chairman of Instruction in Piano
The University of North Carolina

With a Preface by Arthur Loesser
Illustrated by John V. Allcott

HARPER & ROW, PUBLISHERS

New York and Evanston

To my students, who, by being students,
have compelled me to crystallize
these thoughts on
piano playing

Contents

CONTENTS

Preface

by ARTHUR LOESSER

THE pianist has his problems. It is by solving them that he enters upon the delights of piano playing. Why must these problems be? For answer, we must acknowledge that some of them are inherent in the paradoxical nature of the piano itself.

To begin with, the piano appears as one of the most mechanical of all instruments. Fiddlers and pipers are appalled at the levers upon levers that interpose between the source of the piano tone and the player's bodily impulse. Yet this mechanical complexity is no end in itself. Nor is it designed as a means to any sort of automatism. Its real purpose is to provide a tool that will respond with maximum sensitivity to the human touch. Each lever, each regulator, that has been added over the years has enabled the tones to reflect just so much more faithfully the variety of impacts that the hands can produce.

But because of this mechanical complexity, piano playing is always in danger of falling into a dry, prosaic clatter. The player is allowed only the one tiny instant while the hammer is in contact with the string to produce the desired live tone. However, for the clever player that instant is enough. On a good piano the resonance of the tone—its remains, its corpse, if you will—may have a beauty of its own, which he can mold to an exquisite, artistic purpose. To be sure, the pianist must be a sophisticated, canny fellow if he wishes to count as a musician in this way. He will need more than the simpler instincts that guide the singer, for he must know how to cajole, almost to cheat, the music out of the great ironbound structure of the piano.

The piano poses other paradoxes. Unlike the violin, the difficulties of which are apparent from the start, the piano is deceptively easy to play acceptably in the early stages of learning. But to achieve its higher capabilities becomes difficult out of all proportion. Little time goes by before the aspiring pianist runs up against problems of muscular co-ordination, of mental grasp, that fewer and fewer can surmount.

Then, too, we think of the piano as the universal instrument for performers and composers alike. How impressive is the array of saints and heroes of musical creation who have entrusted some of their most valuable thoughts to it! Yet, there have been musicians, some of them great composers, whose affections have been inaccessible to the peculiar genius of the piano. Thus, the piano remains the most practical, the most complete, among instruments, yet the most refractory—ready to frustrate its bunglers, but to reward its craftier, more diligent devotees with a matchless exhilaration.

Fortunately, the prognosis for the pianist's problems is good. Eighty years ago a writer called the piano "the leading musical instrument of Christendom." If it has since declined somewhat from that pre-eminence, the decline may be regarded as extensive rather than intensive. No longer is piano playing generally degraded into a shallow, showy "accomplishment" for genteel young ladies. It is studied by fewer persons today, perhaps, than formerly, but it is studied with much more intelligence and honesty of purpose.

The newer attitude toward piano study has made obsolete some of the older ideas. Inevitably, modern practitioners view its problems from modern perspectives and quite properly pass on to others the benefits of their enlightenment. William Newman is a skillful pianist. What is more, he is a man of thought, enterprise, and experience. He has overcome many a difficulty of his own. He has understood and helped to lighten the difficulties of many others. We do well to hear him with interest and respect.

Cleveland, Ohio, May, 1949

About the Revised
and Enlarged Edition

In her wise little book *On Teaching the Piano* Hetty Bolton reminds teachers to keep up their own growth, then quotes Robert Louis Stevenson: "To hold the same views at forty as we held at twenty is to have been stupefied for a score of years." Well, forty has come and gone since this book was first written. But that was a mere six years ago. Perhaps, then, I shall be pardoned for still holding pretty much to the same views, while claiming only that these have since hatched a new brood of like ones.

In this new edition, "revised" means that many sections were reworded to get in the new ideas or to clarify former ones. The lists of books and music were revamped, too. "Enlarged" refers to two wholly new chapters, one to tie in the book's main points with an illustrated plan for learning new pieces, the other to present two provocative questions of today's teaching methods.

As was hinted in the Author's Foreword, the problem pianist may well be a good one to write on the pianist's problems! At any rate, it has been encouraging to see the book make its way here and abroad, and to find it warmly commended by several front-rankers (including Egon Petri, whose fine ideas I had known).

Hearty thanks are due once more to students and colleagues for valued suggestions; to little Craig (a first addition since the First Edition) for excusing daddy's far-off look at storytelling time; and, of course, to Claire, who saw this thing through again (even to missing more TV shows than I did) with that loyalty and sense of humor only a wife can have.

W.S.N.

Author's Foreword

THE immediate impetus for this book came from a recent lecture-recital tour of colleges and universities in the Midwest, during which I was much impressed by an eager interest in everything that was practical and up to date about piano playing. The intention to write the book goes further back, however. For some time I have been promising students and teachers in my department that I would put down in writing a straightforward account of what I felt "every pianist ought to know." My thought was to supply those essential principles of practice, technique, and musicianly playing that can best be had from a book, leaving the lesson time freer for intangible problems that are better illustrated and tried over "in person."

The actual writing has proved to be one of the most satisfying tasks that I can recall undertaking, no doubt because it relates throughout to experiences that I myself have lived and believed. There is a satisfaction, too, in getting down to earth; in probing problems of everyday concern to student and teacher. Perhaps the very ordinariness of these problems has kept a good many of them from being considered in other books on piano playing. Or perhaps other factors are responsible. In any case, I would hardly be the first to cite their neglect as a characteristic failing among all too many books of this sort. Glib generalizations abound that cannot be translated into practicalities. "The secret of my method" is heralded in prefaces, yet never gets divulged because such a "secret" does not exist outside the aura of the writer's personality.

The main point, I suppose, is that the great artists are rightly too preoccupied with their art to investigate what must seem to them like the mundane details of learning. It is a truism to state that successful performers do not necessarily make knowing teachers. Repeatedly the acknowledged artist, seeking to account for something that his talents enable him to do without effort, attempts to guide others with explanations and procedures that directly contradict basic tenets of the physiologist, the psychologist, and—yes—even the composer.

This charge leads me to what is at least a pretty rationalization and at most a valid justification for this book. I like to see an analogy in Oliver Wendell Holmes's country doctor, who was all the better in his profession for having been a sickly man himself. A Rubinstein or a Horowitz might wonder what the obstacle was, where a lesser man could advise, "Try this; I found it to help when I experienced the same difficulty."

The Pianist's Problems (originally called by the bulkier if catchier title *Are You Wasting Time at the Piano?*) was allowed to "simmer" for several months before publication was undertaken. During those months more students, teachers, and other colleagues from all parts of the country read and commented on the original manuscript than I can possibly list here to thank. They will know how indebted I am to them when they see their extremely useful suggestions incorporated here. However, I do mean to single out the eminent American composer and pianist Arthur Shepherd, and that peerless performer and teacher Arthur Loesser, who have commented so choicely that I have decided to insert their reactions as verbatim quotations where they apply rather than to lose these in the text.

WILLIAM S. NEWMAN

The Pianist's Problems

. . . the ordering of exercises is matter of great consequence to hurt or help; for, as is well observed by Cicero, men in exercising their faculties, if they be not well advised, do exercise their faults and get ill habits as well as good; so there is great judgment to be had in the continuance and intermission of exercises.

Francis Bacon, *The Advancement of Learning*

Introduction

T HE reader must have noticed, in *The Etude* and other favorite magazines of the practicing pianist, how often the same troubled queries reappear: How can memorizing be made easier and more secure? Which exercises yield the best results?

What is to be done about stage fright? Why are some editions better than others? How can the fourth and fifth fingers be strengthened? What produces musicianship? These and many others are perennial questions of the greatest practical importance to student, teacher, and performer. Strange, then, that adequate answers are so hard to find. With all the time and effort devoted to the study of the piano, with all the advances in the psychology of training, with all the special studies that have been conducted, there should be, by now, if not one right answer to each question, at least a preferred answer that will be right for the large majority of pianists.

As a matter of fact, there are preferred answers in almost every instance. They alone do not account for what makes great pianists great; but they can afford substantial help to those of us with average talents who hope to avoid the pitfalls and smooth out the tortuous road from beginner to accomplished pianist. Such answers grow out of the specific research of scholars like Breithaupt and Ortmann, out of the inspired doctrines of teachers like Leschetizky, Matthay, and Busoni, and out of the wide experience of countless students who have had to learn their methods the hard way. The need is to bring these answers together, in one place, and to present them in nontechnical language as a concise, up-to-date, co-ordinated philosophy of piano playing. To meet this need, the present book has been written.

The first four chapters are organized according to the four main problems of any applied music study—Musicianship, Technique, Practice, and Performance. Then follows a chapter illustrating more specifically how these problems may be met in the successive stages of learning. The final chapter considers two highly pertinent questions of teaching method. Of course, a full discussion of piano problems would fill many volumes. Therefore, the emphasis here must be on things that give the most trouble and those that seem to be most basic, or neglected, or controversial. The ideas presented here have been borne out by my own day-by-day experience as performer, teacher, and student, a fact that will perhaps excuse the several references to myself. Some of these ideas represent complete reversals of ideas formerly handed down to me. Many of them will not be found in other books. However, I can hardly claim that the large number of them are either original with me or unique. They also represent, in frequent instances, the experience of my pianist friends in diverse schools throughout the country, and the conclusions reached in various scientific and controlled studies.

To whom, then, is this book primarily addressed? To the student and teacher alike who are eager to make the most of their respective talents; to each in turn, since each must understand the other's problems as well as his own in order to get the fullest view. There are others, too, for whom I hope the book will be of value. Artist performers may be able to pick up a useful pointer here and there; interested parents may gain an insight into the pianist in the making; and piano pedagogy classes may find not only some new blood in the book's ideas but a practical sequence of these ideas such as is necessary in a class text.

One other point should be made now. Except for the beginning year or so (as discussed in the final chapter) what is said here applies in principle and within the limits of comprehension as much to pianists at one age or level as another. Differences in the problems of young and adult students are commonly exaggerated. We tend to underestimate both the interpretative and intellectual powers of the child, on the one hand, and the ability of the adult to learn new skills, on the other. Yet it is remarkable how early and quickly a child can learn to count or transpose, how soon he takes pleasure in the simplest music of Bach and Chopin. As for the adult, his problem lies not, as he supposes, in relative speed of advancement—for he usually learns at least as rapidly as the child—but in his attitude toward his progress. Too often he is impatient because his more mature tastes and interests remain far ahead of his abilities and because he takes too analytical and self-conscious a view of his learning behavior.

Perfectly sound learning may seem very erratic when examined step by step. The student may fail to realize, for example, that the ascent into the higher regions of his skill will not be a steady one. Instead, he must pause time and time again as he reaches temporary limits to the amount of material that he can grasp. At each of these limits he will find himself on a "plateau" where he seems to "bog down" for a while. Actually, the plateau marks the period during which he assimilates what he has just struggled to know. Then, no sooner is the assimilation complete than he must ascend to another level of new material. This may discourage him too, because it tends to upset the security he has just achieved. Yet, such is the stepwise path along which learning progresses.

I. Musicianship

THE phases of musicianship discussed here concern skills and experiences outside the assigned lesson, yet skills and experiences that contribute fundamentally to artistic judgment and technical mastery in performance. Of far-reaching significance to the pianist are the abilities to play by ear, to read at sight, and to participate in ensembles. Much too often these fail to find their way into the lesson because their importance to learning and performance is not understood, or because they are left to general theory and musicianship classes where the special problems of piano playing can hardly receive adequate attention, or simply because the teacher himself is deficient in them. Yet the growing number of successful beginners' books that include musicianship drills, and the increasing place that musicianship courses are taking in the conservatory curriculum, are encouraging evidence of the ever greater attention that problems of musicianship are receiving, from the student's very first lesson to his most advanced coaching.

It was the fashion some years ago to discourage playing at sight or by ear as a distraction, even a harmful influence in the regular, assigned lesson. To be sure, these practices are pleasurable in a way that may tempt the student away from slower, more exacting tasks; and in their very informality they do tend to condone slovenliness, at least in those who fail to develop habits of neatness and precision anyway. But, like the sulfa

5

drugs, when wisely administered in proper doses they may work wonders. It is well to have the student apportion his playing by ear and at sight to, say, the last ten per cent of his practice time, when he will be ready for the diversion that these practices offer and in no danger of cutting deeply into the time for his assigned pieces. Ensemble playing should get at least one session a week. After these projects have been introduced and explained, the teacher need give only a fraction of the lesson to them, ordinarily just enough to make certain they are being followed up correctly.

ON LEARNING TO PLAY BY EAR

The values of being able to play by ear are several. In the first place, there is a marked correlation between this ability and the ability to memorize. Of course, as will be seen, other

factors enter equally into memorizing. Yet, almost invariably, the student who cannot play by ear memorizes slowly or insecurely. Secondly, playing by ear contributes to that elusive quality of good piano playing, fluency. It does this both because it leads to the kind of harmonic grasp that perceives notes in intelligible groups rather than one at a time and because it provides a variety of practical experiences. Finally, by translating to the piano a mental concept that comes via the ear, rather than a printed page that comes via the eye, the student takes active steps to heighten his harmonic, melodic, and rhythmic acuity.

What should be played by ear? Anything and everything that appeals and that can be culled from the memory. This is most likely to include folk-type music, familiar themes from standard classics, and jazz. It is less likely to include contrapuntal or extreme modern music, although the student does no harm in trying to recall these. Improvising, too, has certain values, but it requires special discipline if it is not to fall into stereotyped idioms and progressions that lead nowhere. Do not disavow the kind of balanced diet that includes jazz, which stands out as one important part of our American culture. Day in and day out the contention that jazz players cannot adapt themselves to serious concert music is disproved.

Occasionally the student presents a problem in that he retains tunes very poorly and sometimes remembers nothing at all in its entirety. Perhaps he has never done anything to exercise his musical memory, such as singing around the house. Even so, he is still evincing one kind of musical shortcoming that may or may not be counterbalanced by outstanding strength in other musical attributes. One help for such a student is to provide him with a book of folk and familiar melodies. He can then memorize one of these at a time and supply his own accompaniments. The student's own plea that he is a monotone should generally be discredited. An actual monotone is generally about as rare as an actual case of ptomaine poisoning.

Teachers discover that new students vary widely in their ability to play by ear. Some have trained themselves surprisingly well and merely need guidance in creating more interesting accompaniments and in choosing more purposeful or varied harmony. Others have to struggle even to pick out a one-finger melody. Only too often a student will be playing advanced works without any sense of the aural approach to the piano. In this person's playing the deficiency will crop up in many subtle and unexpected ways, often resulting in halting, unmusical performance.

At this point, Mr. Arthur Loesser, who kindly provided extremely conscientious and helpful reactions to an earlier draft of this book, remarked,

"Check and double check to everything you say about playing by ear. But what will you do with the earnest soul who cannot even get started at it? There are ever so many students, alas, to whom the keyboard is a completely lifeless mechanism, who cannot mentally associate a key with a tone until after they have struck it. Oh, yes, they can learn to play a Chopin Etude sometimes, but they cannot find the "Star-Spangled Banner" in E-flat. What medicine for them?"

My prescription follows in some detail, since playing by ear seems to be a very vague though necessary matter for a good many pianists.

If the student must start in from the beginning to learn to play by ear, then he must have some preparatory work. Since the skill must be not only intuitive but under conscious, intellectual control, an elementary knowledge of scales, keys, intervals, and chords—in short, of the musician's everyday jargon—will come first and can be introduced as outlined here. (Elsewhere I have tried to supply a more general introduction to music theory, styles, and forms, as noted in the listing for *Understanding Music* among Source References on page 164.)

How to build major scales may be taught in two easy stages:

1) Learn the meaning of whole and half steps. Distinguish them by ear; sing them; play them. Always name them as adjacent letters.

2) Build a scale on each of the twelve chromatic tones according to the whole- and half-step pattern 11½ 111½. Do this *a*) on paper, *b*) reciting the successive letter names at the piano, and *c*) singing them away from the piano. In spelling the tones, never repeat or skip a letter, never mix flats and sharps, even though this sometimes means the use of double sharps or flats.

Key relationships may readily be taught by the familiar circle (or clock) of fifths, with emphasis on the "magic number" five:

1) Draw a circle and enter C, representing the key of no accidentals, where noon shows on the clock. Then, counting up a *perfect* fifth each time, enter the sharp keys in the order of 1 to 7 sharps where the corresponding hours would fall on the clock.

2) Similarly, enter the seven flat keys counterclockwise where the numbers 11 to 5 would fall, by counting perfect fifths *down* from C. Note especially the six overlapping or "enharmonic keys (at 5, 6, and 7 on the clock), thus leaving only twelve actual out of fifteen theoretical keys.

3) Determine the order of the sharps themselves (FCGDAEB) and of the flats (the same sequence reversed), again by counting perfect fifths up and down, respectively.

Intervals are best presented as though the lower note is the tonic of a major scale. Since the other tones of the major scale always form a major or perfect interval with the tonic, the upper note of the interval may easily be compared with the inflection it would have in the major scale. Thus, in the augmented sixth B♭-G♯, the G-sharp may be compared with the G-natural that belongs in the major scale of B-flat.

Finally, traditional chord structure is explained with no difficulty to the student who knows his scales. Triads and sevenths may be erected on the root indicated by the Roman numeral or the name for any scale degree simply by selecting every other letter. For instance, in the key of A, the IV or subdominant chord is the chord built on D, the fourth scale degree, and formed in this way: DEF#GA.

For a concentrated, catchall drill that includes chords, intervals, and minor as well as major keys, the student may invent questions along the following pattern, preferably answering them away from the piano:

> *Question.* What are the tones and what intervals do they define in the III triad of the harmonic minor scale of five sharps?
> *Answer.* B, D-sharp, F-double-sharp; major third and major third, totaling an augmented fifth.

The variables in this question are, of course, the choice of triad (from I to VII), of mode (major or any kind of minor), and of the number (one to seven) and kind (sharp or flat) of accidentals.

Students who are woefully weak in the intuitive side of playing by ear may also need the help of other preliminaries such as these:

1) Sight-sing the letter names and conduct the meter of simple melodies like those found in the singing books of the grammar grades. Do this away from the piano, working out the leaps by thinking through the intervening tones.
2) Do the same with familiar melodies from memory. (See below on how to find the starting tone.)
3) At the piano, transpose hymns and folk-tune arrangements such as those found in community songbooks. Choose both near and distant keys.
4) Play basic, cadential chord progressions like the two in Ex. 1, which may be continued clockwise and counterclockwise, respectively, around the circle of keys. Always use the same fingerings and chord positions. Shift octaves as necessary so as to remain at the center of the piano.

These skills may seem far removed from actual piano playing. Yet they have a direct bearing on playing by ear and so contribute in many ways to the rounded musicianship of successful performers.

To gain full command of the keyboard the student should choose a new key, moving clockwise around the circle of fifths, each time he undertakes to play another piece by ear. Still more important, he should make certain that he can count out the

Ex. 1

meter of whatever he plays by ear. The prime necessity for counting as a means to authoritative rhythm in performance will be discussed later. Here the important consideration is the interrelation of meter and chord change in the traditional harmony that the student uses to play by ear. The rule of thumb that requires a change of chord or bass over the bar (that is, from "weak" to "strong" beat) may be familiar enough to him, but he can hardly apply it if he does not know where the bars occur in his tune. Similarly, the correct use of the appoggiatura and other nonharmonic tones depends on metric relationships. Thus, one learns to watch for a tone on the first beat when it is quitted stepwise, up or down, knowing that it will usually sound most convincing when treated as an appoggiatura—that is, as a nonharmonic tone that sideslips into one of the tones of the next chord rather than a harmonic tone in a chord of its own. For instance, at the opening of "Annie Laurie," we ordinarily prefer the second alternative in Ex. 2.

This is also not the place for a review of keyboard harmony, but a few suggestions as to procedure may again be helpful to interested pianists. The usual problem is to recall a tune and to provide it with a correct, if not *the* correct, harmonic accom-

Ex. 2

paniment. The student does well, first, to pick out the tune alone and learn to count it. Pausing to figure out the interval in the "mind's ear" is better than haphazard, hunt-and-peck trial and error. The initial difficulty of determining what tone of the scale the tune starts on is usually met by establishing the chosen key with a simple I-IV-V-I cadence. Then if the tonic chord is played with each of its notes on top in turn, the student will ordinarily hear one of them as the starting tone or a neighbor of the starting tone (most familiar tunes begin on one of the tones of the tonic triad). The student will do best at first to play only the melody in his right hand with an um-pah-pah (bass-chord-chord), *um-pah-um-pah*, or *um-pah-pah-pah* accompaniment in the left. The *um* will ordinarily be the chord root played one to three octaves below the right hand. The *pah* will be the chord complete or, which is often better, the chord minus the tone being played in the melody, its position usually centering around middle C or as near to the right hand as is possible without interference.

It is essential for the student to realize that a strong, satisfactory harmony may be found solely with the use of the I, IV, and V chords, since these define the basic directions of all harmonic movement and since they contain every tone of the scale. If he masters just these primary chords, he will have gone a long way toward meeting the pianist's need for playing by ear. A sensible way for him to approach them is to determine first the focal harmonies at the main structural divisions in the tune, then the intermediary chords, just as he might prepare an English theme by first outlining the idea, then filling in the detail. Actually, there is not much choice. The problem is primarily one of learning to anticipate the "feel" of the proper triad. In the following diagram, which shows the tonic (I) as a chord of repose between the counterbalanced, suspensive chords of the subdominant (IV) and dominant (V), it is apparent that only the first and fifth scale degrees (C and G) are members of more than one chord.

$$
\begin{array}{ccc}
& G\ B\ D & \\
& C\ E\ G & \\
F\ A\ C & & \\
IV & I & V
\end{array}
$$

Each of the other degrees can belong to only one chord (unless it is treated as a chord seventh in descending melodies, which happens most often when the fourth degree is included in the dominant harmony). As for the choice of chords on the first and fifth degrees, sometimes one of these will immediately sound much better than the other to the student; at other times either will do, depending only on personal taste. In Ex. 3, note

that there is little question about the chord for the first C and
G, no question about that for A, and a choice on the final G,
depending on whether a less or more suspensive ending is
preferred.

Ex. 3

After the student shows a musicianly command of the fundamental harmonies, which chiefly means sensing the full and half
cadences, avoiding parallelisms between IV and V, and choosing

Ex. 4

the chord that best accommodates the melodic outline, he may
attempt other harmonies. To such a student certain additional
procedures are recommended. These should be introduced in
easy stages and in their approximate order of frequency or need:

First come the familiar full-cadence formulas, especially ii-V-I and I_4^6-V-I or their variants, as at the end of "Old Folks at Home" and of "Battle Hymn of the Republic" in Ex. 4. These formulas quickly become identified with characteristic melodic closes, the 2-2-1 and 8-7-8 scale progressions in this same example being very common ones.

Second comes the principal dominant embellishment, the major triad or seventh chord erected on II. This secondary dominant (V of V) permits temporary modulations to the dominant key and more varied half cadences, as at the midpoint of Haydn's "Emperor" theme in Ex. 5.

iii   vi   V   of   V

Ex. 5

Next, the student may try his hand at the use of other dominant embellishments ("applied" dominants), or rather at the use of any of the triads I to vi, preceded by *its own* dominant harmony. In effect, he will be establishing temporary dominant-tonic relationships between weak and strong beats at suitable points in the melody. Although this procedure soon becomes obnoxious in simple folk songs, it furnishes a valuable guide to students learning to play by ear. Stated briefly, any melody tone that falls on a strong beat may be harmonized as root, 3d, 5th, or even 7th, of a major or minor chord in the original key (or as an appoggiatura of any of these) provided the melody permits the particular dominant of that chord to occur on the preceding weak beat (or beats).

More explicitly, in this last procedure these observations will normally apply:

1) To find the temporary tonics, systematically test each strong-beat tone to determine what major or minor chord within the key it might be the root of, what the 3d, and so on. Thus, in the key of G, B might be treated as the root of the iii, the 3d of the I, or the 5th of the vi chord. Any of these may be selected if its own dominant (that is, the major chords on F-sharp, D, and B, respectively, in the examples just cited) does not clash unintelligibly with the foregoing melody.

2) Foreign accidentals (altered tones) will be required for the embellishing dominants (thus, the E-major chord is the dominant of vi in C) but not for the temporary tonics (disregarding the possibility of "borrowed" tones).

3) Strong and weak beats are determined by the bar line and the tempo. In slower music, the first beat of a measure will be a strong beat (as will the third beat in four-quarter meter) and the other beats will be weak. In faster music, corresponding relationships occur in the grouping of the measures. Thus, in the waltz and quick march time, the embellishing dominant will often occupy an entire "weak" measure so that the temporary tonic and its applied dominant alternate in two-measure groups. Greater harmonic stability and smoothness is achieved, in any case, by placing the embellishing dominant as far back in its measure as possible.

4) Descending melodies offer more possibilities than ascending ones, since the normal resolution of the dominant 7th (or even 9th) is downward, a fact that requires constant supervision. To illustrate dominant embellishments, the second phrase of "Annie Laurie" may be varied as in Ex. 6.

These generalized procedures represent the harmonic limits most pianists are likely to reach or need to reach, in so far as playing by ear affects the success of performance. Idiomatic progressions, like the passing six-four and four-three chords or the special handlings of the leading tone, are readily learned but they apply much more to four-part harmonizations of the chorale type. So with modulations, such as the approach to the bass of the I_4^6 chord in the new key through the diminished seventh chord a half step below, which is chiefly useful in improvisation.

Transposition to any and every key should figure as an integral part of all playing by ear. Fortunately, many beginners are required to play their early pieces in at least half a dozen keys. It is true, this practice will not assure them of the skill that enabled Brahms to transpose the piano part of Beethoven's *Kreutzer* Sonata from A to A-sharp at a moment's notice. But it will help them to sense inherent musical relationships and not

Ex. 6

just the mechanics of a single arrangement of notes on the keyboard. Incidentally, one American college now expects its recitalists to be ready to transpose at least one piece to any other key that is requested, right at the program!

The student will do well to keep a dated record of what he plays by ear, listing title and key and noting any difficulties that may arise so that they can be discussed with the teacher; also so that he may realize which keys need the most attention.

SIGHT READING FOR PROFIT AND PLEASURE

Much is to be gained by regular sight reading. First of all, there are the obvious advantages of being able to read fluently at sight. Fluency in this skill is a prime requisite of the professional pianist, especially of the accompanist, teacher, ensemble player, and radio staff member. Fluency in this skill gives the student a chance to learn a new piece before he tires of it. Besides, nothing is likely to discourage him more than an initial struggle with a maze of incomprehensible notes, notes that may actually present no technical problem once he has learned to read them. Fluency also means an open door to a great deal of pleasurable music that he would otherwise miss. And, to put it mildly, the matter of pleasure in music must not be overlooked! We sometimes get so serious, even anxious, about our music study that we forget, after all, that one of the main values of music is the pleasure it can afford.

A second main value to be gained from sight reading is this. Sight reading enables the student to acquaint himself with a wide variety of basic literature, both original and arranged, that he cannot hope to cover in his own study and performance. Finally, sight reading introduces him to a wealth of technical, stylistic, and interpretative experiences that contribute directly to the physical and artistic grasp of the pieces he sets out to learn.

Sight reading should be gone at systematically, with a panorama of literature mapped out in advance. Naturally, while he is just starting in, the student must content himself with persistent reading from his own and other beginners' books. Sight

reading of much elementary material should be a main ingre-
dient in his early training, anyway. After about a year he will
be able to look into the easiest of the classics, the little preludes,
sonatinas, and other short pieces that the great composers were
thoughtful enough to leave to us. Eventually, he may begin
to go through the standard literature, the Beethoven Sonatas, the
Bach "Forty-eight," the Debussy Preludes, the late pieces of
Brahms, and all those other classics that comprise the pianist's
daily bread. Taking this approach, the student who can perform,
say, the *Pathétique* Sonata of Beethoven may be expected to
cover the entire standard literature in as little as four years, with
only a few minutes of reading a day. His chief problem, if he
cannot afford to buy much of this music for himself as discussed
further on, will be to find a library from which he can borrow.

The student will do best if he covers a complete volume at a
time, choosing according to the limitations of his technique and
musical understanding, transferring from one era and style to
another for variety and a balanced diet, and keeping a dated
record of what he plays. Certainly, if he is studying a Mozart
sonata, a Chopin prelude, or any other piece that is one among
many of its kind, he will enhance his general perspective and
his understanding of that piece by reading all of its fellows in
the same volume.

He will profit still further if he is asked to write brief but
careful comments in a "sight-reading notebook." His object here
should be not so much to make subjective generalizations, such
as "It's pretty" or "I don't like it," as to single out, objectively
and within his limitations, those traits that distinguish the one
piece from any other. For example, in what ways—melodic,
rhythmic, harmonic, dynamic, textural, formal, technical, or
other—does Schumann's *Carnaval* differ from his *Symphonic
Studies*, or, to take a more extreme example, Debussy's *Maid
With the Flaxen Hair* from Handel's *Harmonious Blacksmith*?

If he can discern only the recurrence of a motive as against the variation principle in the Schumann works, or the difference in harmonic color between the music of Debussy and Handel, the student will have made important observations of his own. And that is the object of his comments: to awaken his powers of observation. Just the knowledge that he must have something to say when he completes his reading compels him to observe what he is doing.

As is only too well known, pianists, who have everything laid out literally in black and white before them, can go along quite oblivious of the music they are playing. So can other instrumentalists, for that matter, though they ordinarily have opportunities unknown to the pianist for extensive pitch and tone control, opportunities that at least encourage attention to the performance if not to the music itself. The violinist has to attend to pitch, for example, since there are no frets to guide him on his finger board. Of course, all players of wind and bowed-stringed instruments have another obligation unknown to the pianist; they must make judicious use of their ability to swell, diminish, and sustain a tone at will.

With regard to the technique of sight reading, a few suggestions should prove useful. The prime difficulty in sight reading is almost always rhythm rather than notes. Although there are eighty-eight notes on the piano, and these are combined in a nearly inexhaustible variety of harmonies, the fact remains that the notes will invariably appear in fixed places on the staff and on the keyboard. Rhythm, on the other hand, is much more elusive. To be sure, the number of different note values and signs in common use is comparatively small, but these are arranged in varied combinations that are neither tangible nor predictable in the way that notes are.

The performer has to do more than read rhythms; he has to sense them inwardly and in advance in order to understand and play them properly. It is at once evident that accurate counting is a *sine qua non* of sight reading wherever there can be any possibility of confusion. Sight reading should be done at a tempo that permits at least 80 per cent of the notes to be played correctly. It also must be done musically, reproducing as nearly as possible the intention of the composer. Therefore, if getting in 80 per cent of the notes means playing too slowly for the intent of the music, easier music will have to be read until the skill improves. Naturally the level of technique sets an upper limit.

Reading notes rapidly presents much the same problems as reading words rapidly. We are helped in prose by seeing combinations of letters as syllables, combinations of syllables as words, even combinations of words as whole phrases. Similarly we are helped in music, always depending on the extent of our intuitive and intellectual command of harmony, by seeing combinations of tones as chords and combinations of chords as familiar progressions. (In this way sight reading can actually become an approach to piano study, as discussed in our final chapter.) No wonder that the more unfamiliar the idiom, as in today's music or a foreign language, the slower the music or words must be read.

Certainly, looking ahead and quick mental recording of the image are major factors in rapid reading. To develop these skills among slow readers in school or prospective airplane spotters, flash cards are often used. Without such aids the pianist can mainly try consciously to look at least a measure ahead (depending on the tempo) and not simply keep his eyes glued on the staff notes he is then playing. If successful, he really does two things at once: reads ahead and plays *from memory* what has just been read. To prove that such is possible try a related experiment. Play the leading voice in any canon (as in the finale of Franck's Violin Sonata) and get someone not looking at it to whistle the imitating voice at the right time interval. By hearing one part while he whistles the other he clearly is not thinking only of one thing at a time.

Here Mr. Loesser inserts,

"Of course. In fact, I often say, 'In music you must never think of what you are doing.' Startled query: 'Well, what *must* you think of?' Answer: 'What you are *going* to do.'"

This principle also suggests that a good sight reader will have sufficient feel for the keyboard so that he does not have to look at the keys themselves as he plays.

Sometimes the visual reaction speed can be improved by setting the metronome to the proper tempo and then sticking with it, come hell or high water. The use of the metronome in this way may induce a degree of "faking." But actually, a degree of faking, if it is the intelligent kind that singles out the correct harmonic outlines and omits only relatively unessential tones, is an important part of successful sight reading, as any professional will readily confess. Sight reading in ensemble music achieves the same results even better than the metronome, both because the players feel even more impelled to go on (the violinist in an orchestra must hang on for dear life because he knows the orchestra will never go back for him if he alone gets lost) and because they can be more musical when they have rhythmic freedom. And that brings us to another contributive factor in musicianship, ensemble playing.

JOIN AN ENSEMBLE AND BE MUSICAL

The pianist who has thus far failed to play in ensembles truly does not know how much pleasure he has missed. It would certainly be no exaggeration to say that most experienced pianists find greater actual musical enjoyment in ensemble than in solo playing. This fact brings up the pleasure value of music again. Ensemble playing is usually so much fun, socially as well as musically, that once the habit is under way the student rarely needs any further inducements to keep it up. Music thrives in society, so that "breaking the ice" is about the only obstacle to getting students interested. Inertia has to be surmounted in the matters of making appointments to meet, finding a place to rehearse, and borrowing scores and parts. I ordinarily take part of the first studio recital that my students give each semester to overcome this inertia in them. We assemble at the ensemble shelves of the school library, where I first introduce them to the music and to each other. Then I stand right by until they have committed themselves to definite appointments for four-hand

duets at one or two pianos, in rooms known to be available at set times. When we follow up these arrangements by crowding around two pianos to sample some pieces, the ice is broken and the interest aroused.

Piano duets are, of course, only one branch of ensemble playing. But, where instrumentalists other than pianists are scarce, duets can go a long way toward meeting the needs of ensemble playing. Both the original music for four hands and the splendid standard arrangements should be played. It may come as a surprise to some to learn that Schubert's one-piano duets include works like the *Grand Duo* in C and the *Lebensstürme*, works that are quite as extended and dramatic as his great Symphony in C and his two-cello Quintet in C. These, to my mind, are of more consistent worth and inspiration than any of his solo piano music. Mozart's great F major Sonata for one-piano duet and his sparkling D major Sonata for two pianos (as well, of course, as the piano concertos with the orchestra part reduced for second piano) are, again, finer than any of his solo sonatas, in my estimation.

Although the same cannot be said for the duets of Haydn, Beethoven, Schumann, or Mendelssohn, there are a sufficient number of other great works to keep the student occupied for a long while and to fill a number of exciting programs of original duets, among them the Variations, Op. 23, by Brahms, the one- and two-piano sonatas by Hindemith, the delightful sonatas or suites by Kuhlau, Fauré, and Debussy, and even some early Elizabethan music. Fortunately, the literature is good right from the beginning stage, thanks to series like that of Diller and Quaile, in which the pupil's part is made much easier than the teacher's.

As for arrangements, it is common knowledge that one of the best ways to explore the great masterpieces of chamber music and the orchestra is through duet reductions. In their humble way, the excellent arrangers, employed notably for Edition Peters, made an invaluable contribution when they thus supplied the best of all the great masters from Bach to Bruckner. In music schools every effort should be made to stock the libraries with such arrangements.

If the pianist is to join with players on other instruments, the most common mediums will be the piano trio (piano, violin, and cello) and the duo for piano with one string or wind instrument. The original literature is similarly ample for these combinations and broad in the range of its difficulty. The arrangements are not so ample and are more likely to be of less than first-class quality. However, even the albums of hackneyed old favorites have their uses, be the piano parts ever so subordinate. The student will speak up soon enough if he is bored.

The importance of ensemble playing to sight reading, exploration of the classics, and sheer musical pleasure has already been mentioned. One other contribution, inherent in the very nature of this practice, has still to be stated. That is the sensitivity that ensemble playing awakens to musical values. Just the quick shift from accompaniment to solo to *tacet* that each player must constantly make in skillfully contrived ensemble music trains him to single out what does predominate and subordinate what does not.

Surprisingly, though loud playing seems to be congenital among pianists, the common fault in ensembles with other types of instruments (though not in piano duets) is to regard everything as an accompaniment to be subdued. Even when pianists do recognize a solo as such they often lack the courage to assert their part. In this, they may not realize that modern chamber music grew out of compositions by Haydn, Mozart and their forerunners, in which the piano had all of the solo and the strings played an entirely subordinate role. Even the *Kreutzer* Sonata by Beethoven was originally called a sonata for piano with violin obbligato! Nothing is quite so musically frustrating as to hear one of the fine "piano and violin" sonatas by Brahms played as though the piano had only an accompaniment, its part being at least as important as the violin's. To be sure, there is the other extreme. But I am simply passing by the brash pianist who drowns out his cohorts unmercifully or the well-meaning accompanist who tries to attach melodic significance to a purely harmonic background.

As elsewhere, rhythm looms as the biggest challenge for ensemble players. This is of course to be expected since the very act of playing together depends on rhythmic agreement. And as al-

ways, counting aloud and the use of the metronome are basic
props, at least until the players manage to stay together. Even
then, the metronome may be a powerful aid in giving over-all
continuity to the performance, as will be discussed later and as is
well known to experienced chamber music organizations.

MUSIC AND BOOKS—THE TOOLS OF THE PROFESSION

Under the general heading of musicianship one other topic
must be included. That is the importance to the developing student of collecting a basic library. This topic might have been

considered elsewhere but it fits equally well here, since the basic
library furnishes a prime means of cultivating musicianship,
just as it furnishes a fund of literature from which he can draw
the pieces he studies, the pieces he plays for recreation, and the
pieces he examines to broaden his musical culture. As soon as
the student shows promise of continuing interest, the possibility
should be discussed with him and perhaps with his parents, too
(since it will involve a substantial cash outlay), of buying in one
lump purchase those works that represent the cornerstones of
piano literature, those works that would be essential to his musicianly pleasures were he to be stranded on the proverbial desert
isle.

Several advantages are to be gained thereby. First, the student is supplied at once with resources constantly at hand for exploration, study, and profitable enjoyment. These will be basic to him because they represent the greatest music for his instrument, the music that has continually influenced other musicians, and the music that is most often performed and cited. Second, the student may very well effect a major economy by buying this much music at once. There is the obvious fact that savings up to 300 and 400 per cent may be made by buying the complete volume of any one type of piece (for instance, all the twenty-seven Chopin Etudes) rather than one at a time, as the need arises. But, in addition, dealers are frequently glad to make a discount for a purchase of this size.

Third, a rounded basic library is an insurance against conspicuous gaps in the student's repertoire. Of course, a careful teacher will make periodic checks to ascertain and eliminate those gaps, but the student's own explorations are still the best way of discovering them. Fourth, a rounded basic library is also an insurance against unbalanced tastes—a passion for Debussy and a distaste for Chopin, for example. The dilettante appreciator may argue that he likes what he likes, but the career musician should be discouraged from this view. As a man in the field he should make it his business to understand and really like the best music of every era, or else find out wherein he, not the composer, lacks.

Finally, the student who makes such a lump purchase has an opportunity and an inclination to choose with care the editions he gets. Editions that are inaccurate, badly reproduced, or poorly edited can be very discouraging and very harmful to the student. Each work must be considered separately, since good and bad editions are to be found in the catalogues of almost all publishers. The pronounced swing toward *Urtext* editions—that is, editions in which the music has been reproduced exactly as the composer left it and without additions—is a healthy sign. However, that swing may have gone too far from the student's standpoint. For example, I would almost rather entrust my students to the old Bülow-Lebert edition of Beethoven's Sonatas than to the *Urtext*, in which Beethoven's inconsistencies, especially in the matter of staccatos, slurs, and dynamic signs, can produce no end of confusion. Almost rather, that is, because the Bülow-Lebert edition goes too far the other way, even to making consistent numerous details that were never meant to be so.

The Bach *Urtext* editions are a little easier to use since Bach inserted virtually no editorial markings in his music, thus giving no occasion for such inconsistencies. Even so, much experience with Bach is needed to surmise his probable tempo, expressive, and stylistic intentions unaided. Furthermore, in the music from William Byrd to Beethoven and even Chopin, and especially in the music of Bach, the question of the correct performance of ornaments continually arises. Here, if anywhere, authoritative, modern editorial advice is needed. Nothing is quite so badly misrepresented as the ornament solutions offered in many of the older editions and still in some of the present ones.

There follows a suggested list for a basic library, with at least one out of several good publishers and editions recommended in each instance. It would be tempting to add other standard masterworks, but then the list would quickly skyrocket out of all proportions. The two books at the head of the list deal respectively with musical subject matter and composers and are currently the most practical and authoritative of their types published in this country. The whole of this list may be had for approximately one hundred and seventy-five dollars as this is written. Readers in and about the largest cities, especially New York, Boston, Philadelphia, Chicago, and Los Angeles, should not overlook the possibility of getting standard music and music books in good used condition at one of the numerous "half-price" music exchanges. The procurement of this much music gives a good opportunity to show the student how to care for it properly. He would do well to provide covers for it, house it in organized fashion, and even maintain a catalogue file of what he has. He should also be warned that the loss of music may mean much more than the cost of replacement. It may mean the loss of invaluable fingerings and other personal markings when he wants to relearn a piece.

A Basic Library of Books and Music for Pianists

Books

Willi Apel: *Harvard Dictionary of Music* (latest edition); Harvard University Press.

Baker's Biographical Dictionary of Musicians (latest edition); G. Schirmer.

(Further books are recommended in the Source References on pages 163 and 164, including *Music for the Piano* by Friskin and Freundlich, which can be of much help in the choice of pieces and editions during the further building of the library.)

Music

J. S. Bach: *Concerto* in F minor; Peters (*Urtext* annotated by Teichmueller). *English Suites* in 1 or 2 vols., *French Suites* in 1 or 2 vols., *Partitas* in 1 or 2 vols., *Toccatas, Two-Part Inventions,* and *Three-Part Sinfonias* in 1 or 2 vols., *The Well-Tempered Clavier* (Books I and II); Kalmus (*Urtext* annotated by Bischoff) or Peters (*Urtext* annotated variously by Kreutz, Kroll, Landshoff, Soldan, and others).

Beethoven: *Concertos* Nos. 3, 4, and 5; Kalmus or Peters. *Sonatas* in 2 or 3 vols.; Associated Board Edition (Tovey) or Kalmus (*Urtext*). *Variations* in 2 vols.; Kalmus. *Various Pieces*; Henle, Kalmus, or Peters.

Brahms: *Piano Works* (at least the first two volumes when published in three); Kalmus, Peters, or G. Schirmer.

Chopin: *Ballades, Etudes, Impromptus, Mazurkas, Nocturnes, Polonaises, Preludes, Scherzos and Fantasy, Sonatas, Waltzes;* The Fryderyk Chopin Institute (an important Polish edition by Paderewski and others), Oxford (Ganche), or Peters (Scholz).

Debussy: *Children's Corner, Estampes, Etudes* in 2 vols., *Images* (First and Second Series), *Preludes* in 2 vols.; Durand.

Handel: *Suites* in 2 vols.; Kalmus or Peters.

Haydn: *Sonatas* in 4 vols.; Peters (*Urtext* annotated by Martienssen). *Various Pieces;* Kalmus or Peters.

Liszt: *Etudes* variously collected in 2 or 3 vols., *Hungarian Rhapsodies* in 2 vols.; G. Schirmer. *Original Pieces* in 2 vols.; Peters.

Mendelssohn: *Piano Works* in 5 vols. (including *Songs Without Words*); Augener.

Mozart: *Concertos* in D minor (K. 466), A major (K. 488), and C minor (K. 491); Peters. *Original Duets;* Peters. *Sonatas* in 1 or 2 vols.; Henle (*Urtext* annotated by Lampe), Kalmus (*Urtext,* or edited edition by Bartok), Presser (important new edition of the *Urtext* annotated by Broder). *Various Pieces;* Henle (*Urtex* annotated by Lampe), Kalmus (*Urtext*), Peters (*Urtext*). *Variations;* Kalmus.

Domenico Scarlatti: (60) *Sonatas;* Kalmus (*Urtext* of contemporary copies), G. Schirmer (*Urtext* of contemporary copies, annotated by Kirkpatrick, 2 vols.).

Schubert: *Fantasias, Impromptus, Moments Musicaux,* and *Various Pieces* in 2 vols.; Kalmus. *Original Duets* in 4 vols.; Peters. *Sonatas* in 2 vols.; Kalmus.

Schumann: *Piano Works* in 6 vols.; Kalmus.

ADDITIONAL RECOMMENDATIONS

Representative collections (including Baroque and Modern!) by the other composers mentioned in the descriptive list of the Four Main Eras of Keyboard Music on pages 130 to 131. Sonatas for violin and piano, piano trios, and other chamber music with piano by the great masters. Bach's 371 *Harmonized Chorales.* Beethoven's *Nine Symphonies* arranged for four hands at one piano. Piano-vocal scores of Mozart's *Don Giovanni,* Verdi's *Otello,* Wagner's *Tristan and Isolde,* and Brahms' *German Requiem.*

II. Technique

TECHNIQUE is understood here in the limited sense of phys-ical agility. It is usually what is meant when we hear the earthy colloquialism "he plays a lot of piano." The desire for a "big" and fluent technique has occasioned so much discussion

and consumed so much time and energy that any further men-tion of the subject must be approached with trepidation. Yet, paradoxically, it is precisely that flood of attention that underlies some of the chief remarks to be made here. Sometimes, when the accumulation of material about any topic has been too great—as was the problem when Ernest Newman wrote about Wagner, and Hindemith about written harmony—the best new contri-bution is a reconsideration of the evidence, a sloughing off of excess baggage, and a righting of false notions.

31

A fundamental, practical consideration in any discussion of technique should be physical limitations and capabilities. Do we bear these in mind when we organize our practice? Not sufficiently. Just as any young lady will dress so as to draw attention to her more attractive features and away from any less attractive ones, so every pianist must take stock of himself, make the most of what he has, and try not to run afoul of his shortcomings. Make no mistake about this—every pianist has shortcomings, if only because the physical advantage that makes one passage easy is often the disadvantage that makes another hard. For example, long fingers frequently help in wide stretches but get in their own way in close, chromatic passages.

In any case, we must realize that we have to get along with the equipment that was given us. Fortunately, the literature for piano is so extensive that one can usually select programs suitable to his particular technique, without serious sacrifice of his musical interests. Natural bodily grace, the general nervous structure, the size and shape of the hand, the length and web of the fingers, "breaking" at the finger joints, and muscular flexibility—any or all of these may vary widely and represent by far the most important differences between one person's technical capabilities and another's.

Carl Seashore, best known for his widely used tests of musical talent, has developed a motor test that purports to measure technical capability. It records the number of times the wrist can tap per second and, like the talent tests, is claimed to apply equally to all persons whether they have had musical training or not. Even to the extent that this ability can be measured by eye and ear, I have noted among my students a marked correlation between tapping speed and technical fluency. Of course, all this is not to deny the importance of other factors in the building of a secure technique. Technical fluency and capability are hardly synonymous with technical achievement, which requires, besides a good hand, an intelligent approach to technical problems and the usual perspiration that figures in all achievement.

We are repeatedly reminded, though rarely with concrete remedies, that we tend to regard technique as an end in itself instead of a means to musical ends. I remember calling on a prominent cellist whose main advice was that "technique is everything. What you must have, my boy, is technique, more technique, and more technique!" I also seem to remember a cellist in a Dickens novel who practiced scales all day long and did so because he found his satisfaction in the exercise itself. Most of us, however, really mean to be in the field of music for music's sake. The big question, then, is whether or not we are taking the right means to achieve this end.

DO FORMAL STUDIES SERVE THEIR PURPOSE?

The conviction has grown in recent years among numerous teachers and performers that pianists often go "overboard" in the use of exercises. They glorify the exercise to the point where it is done as a matter of course and for its own sake, quite apart from the goal it should prepare. Not that anyone questions the basic need for exercises and drills. The question is simply this: Are we choosing exercises that will meet that need or are we merely doing any and all exercises on the very treacherous assumption that somehow, somewhere, whatever we do will apply?

It is hard to think of another field in which a complete formal program of extracurricular conditioning is similarly maintained alongside the main study. I have frequently encountered the assertion, though not in the field of music, that each person gets enough exercise for his chosen pursuit directly from the activities that the pursuit itself requires. This applies equally to mental and physical activities. The typist keeps up and improves her typing primarily by typing the daily work allotted to her; the errand boy builds up his necessary stamina simply by running errands; the certified public accountant keeps "in trim" by figuring his accounts. Athletes, too, have come more and more to train by reproducing as nearly as possible the circumstances of the contests they will be entering.

Even in the early stages of these pursuits it is doubtful that the beginner does better, if as well, to train on abstract exercises rather than problems that grow out of his actual experience. It is doubtful, for example, that the typist who drills by the hour on "Now is the time for all good men . . ." learns to type as soon as the one who starts in with the newer drills based on real-life correspondence and manuscripts. Yet the host of pianists, by and large, sticks faithfully to its formal program of the Czerny *Art of Finger Dexterity*, Clementi *Gradus ad Parnassum*, Cramer *Selected Studies*, Hanon *Daily Exercises*, and Pischna *Finger Studies*, enjoying the exhilaration of the ascetic who contemplates the finer things that lie beyond.

For most of Pischna, Hanon, and the like, there is really little excuse. In fact, a kind of psychological lethargy accounts for the great loyalty to their deadly monotonous compilations. The teacher has almost no explaining to do, the student has very little note reading to worry him, and the mind is free to wander into subjects far removed while the required practice minutes tick by. No harm is done, no tempers are ruffled, and—alas!— little or no good is accomplished. For Czerny and his contemporaries there is more justification because much of their music has great charm and some of it real depth.

The vital point, however, is that the practice of a Czerny study leads mainly to the perfection of that Czerny study rather than to Beethoven or Chopin or composers in general. The way to learn Beethoven is first of all to practice Beethoven. The practice of Czerny can help Beethoven only when an identical passage occurs in both, and such practice can mean the wasting of a lot of valuable time. The psychologists will corroborate this statement with, "Why, of course that's so; you musicians are slow to make that discovery. We reached that conclusion when we generally discarded the old theory of transfer of training." The old theory said that mathematics and chess were food for the brain, but now we know that the study of these only makes mathematicians and chess players. We still hear that Latin is a valuable course because it helps with English grammar. There *are* basic principles in Latin that actually carry over, but if that were the only reason for studying Latin, how much easier it would be just to study in English the roots, construction, and syntax that apply.

The main fallacy in adhering to Czerny *et al.* lies, it seems to me, in the illusion that piano practice means the development of the piano-playing muscles in general. But it does not. It means developing specific muscular co-ordinations to meet specific situations. There are woodsmen and athletes who can squeeze any pianist's hand to a pulp. But their splendid strength means nothing at the piano, for, unless they have practiced the act, they can barely set down five fingers in a row. One learns only what he practices. Each technical feat must be learned separately. Technique does not generalize. The most that can happen in general is that the pianist will acquire enough specific experiences to enable him to meet almost whatever confronts him. This would suggest that Czerny can at least supply the pianist with further experiences, though, here again, common sense dictates that if our main interest lies in performing other music, the other music is where we should seek our experience.

Now, having stated my case against the regular use of studies for the sake of exercise, I hasten to add this brief but important qualification: There are indeed times when a certain study will answer a special need very well. A study may be found that counteracts a peculiar mannerism or strengthens a conspicuous weakness. That, in fact, is why most of the well-known exercises were written. Then it should be practiced, but only as needed and not on general principle. (This is said notwithstanding the well-known fact that when Paderewski went to Leschetizky he was put on nothing but Czerny for a year.) Meanwhile, the student must remember that there are other, usually more efficient, ways of meeting actual technical requirements.

MAKING THE MOST OF SCALES AND OTHER DRILLS

Many teachers have come to feel that the careful practice of certain basic drills will suffice for all warm-up and extracurricular technical requirements. Some have invented their own drill sequences, as elaborate and useless as Hanon can be. Others have singled out the standard drills of all pianists, five of which are indeed basic: trills, scales, arpeggios, octaves, and double notes.

Ex. 7

These five exercises, practiced in standard rhythms, have one argument immediately in their favor. They do repeatedly occur, exactly as they may be practiced, in a great deal of piano music written from the early 1600's to the late 1800's. They are much less likely to occur, say, in Hindemith, Bartok, or Milhaud, and thus are presumably less applicable in contemporary music.

Liszt and Paderewski are two among a number of the world's great pianists who reportedly concluded that the simple trill is the fundamental piano exercise. A simple and quick way to practice the trill is as follows: With the hands playing together, place the thumbs on g and c'. Begin the trill of the first and second fingers slowly, in triplet rhythm, as in Ex. 7.

Gradually increase the speed, "locomotive" style, dropping the triplet rhythm when it gets too fast, until the maximum even speed is attained. Continue this as smoothly as possible until the palms seem to tire, which may be not more than a minute if the small hand muscles (lumbricales) operate the fingers as is shortly recommended. The remaining fingers may be played similarly in contrary motion in the order 4-5, 2-3, and 3-4, so as to give them the best chance to rest in between trills. The other trill positions that result from doing the same exercise a half step higher each time are useful, too. Moreover, each group of three fingers—1-2-3,

Ex. 8

3-4-5, 2-3-4—may be exercised in a similar manner equally applicable to many musical situations. This last drill may start as in Ex. 8.

After the rudiments of scales and arpeggios have been shown to him in C major, it seems best for the student to learn these drills in all the keys, major and minor, at the same time. Even beginners seem to progress more rapidly and more securely with this perspective of the whole, based on over-all principles of fingering, than if they master each key before progressing to the next. However, since there is not time to do all of them each day, the keys should be rotated throughout the circle over fairly brief periods of time. For example, the following schedule fills one

week at the rate of two major and two parallel (rather than relative) minor keys per day:

DAILY KEY CHART

Mon.	C—c	F#(G♭)—f#
Tues.	G—g	D♭(C#)—c#
Wed.	D—d	A♭—a♭(g#)
Thurs.	A—a	E♭—e♭(d#)
Fri.	E—e	B♭—b♭(a#)
Sat.	B(C♭)—b	F—f

The student may conveniently follow the same schedule for
his playing by ear and his drill exercises.

Here, then, are some over-all principles of fingering that
should help to avoid the need for individual scale fingerings.
Since all major and minor scale forms contain seven notes in each
octave, the main problem is how to divide each into three plus
four fingers. In other words, which two notes will the thumb fall
on? The answer is best given for the outward direction of the
scale (right hand to the right and left to the left). Then the
thumb plays the first white key after any black key(s), except
for B-flat and E-flat harmonic minor in the left hand, when the
third finger must follow the second finger. The thumb also plays
the tonic of all white-tonic scales (or arpeggios). But the second
finger starts all black-tonic scales, by common practice. It "rounds
the corner" best even though another finger may land on the
next tonic. To play the scales in the opposite direction simply
use the same fingering in reverse (except for obvious changes
when the right hand plays F- and C-sharp melodic minor).

The chief fingering problem that arpeggios raise lies in the
choice between third or fourth finger, since both the thumb and
second finger always play, and the use of the fifth is self-evident.
There are justifiable disagreements on this choice, based on differences in relative finger lengths from one player to the next.

However, the most common method is to use the fourth finger instead of the third only when the outermost pair of tones in the chord (counting from the thumb) are two white keys not more than a major third apart, or a black and a white key a minor third apart. Many players also use the fourth when the black and the white key are a major third apart in first-inversion chords. These three uses of the fourth finger are shown in Ex. 9:

Ex. 9

When the chord to be arpeggiated has two white keys and one black key, the position starting on the black key has two possible fingerings, since it can be played as part of either white-key position. Thus in the D major triad the second position, with the right hand ascending from f♯, may be fingered 2-3-1-2 or 4-1-2-4, as in Ex. 10. For the sake of uniformity, it seems preferable and

Ex. 10

just as easy always to use the fingering of the position that begins on the lowest white key in the triad, which would be 2-3-1-2 in the example cited. Further applications of this principle are shown in Ex. 11. (Note, however, that as in black-tonic scales, the second finger is commonly used on the bottom, starting black key in the right hand, or the top one in the left hand, of arpeg-

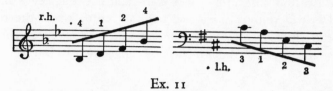

Ex. 11

gios with one black key, regardless of the subsequent fingering.)

Beside certain faults in the finger, hand, and arm action that are to be discussed, unsure fingering and failure to cover the

Ex. 12

notes properly often explain weak scales and arpeggios. An intelligent corrective is supplied by playing these exercises in simultaneous blocks of notes or "clusters," according to the grouping of the fingers. From a learning standpoint, this is like conceiving groups of letters as syllables. In Ex. 12, the D major and E-flat harmonic minor scales are shown grouped and fingered for both the left and right hands. Similarly, the three positions of the E major arpeggio will be played as in Ex. 13. A feeling for the

Ex. 13

shape or mold of the cluster is best induced either by playing the clusters *a*) staccato with wrist action and no give in the fingers (as in the playing of octaves), or *b*) legato, separating the thumb so that it alternates with the remaining block of fingers in each cluster, as in Ex. 14.

Ex. 14

Each hand should be mastered separately, after which the clusters may be tried hands together. When the student sees how and why the scale clusters do not coincide in the two hands, he will be able to cope better with the conflicting fingering that results from playing the scales in parallel motion. Occasionally he should return to the clusters to renew their feel. This feel is also helped, as in sight reading, by trying never to look at the keyboard, even during arpeggios! For proof recall the secure grasp of the keys ("position technique") by most blind pianists.

Here, too, are some general principles for fingering scales in thirds. There is fairly wide agreement on the C major scale,

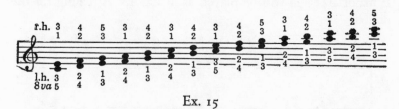

Ex. 15

which may be played as in Ex. 15. A variety of fingerings, however, has been advocated for the scales with one or more accidentals. It is my belief that the simplicity of using one fingering for all major and natural minor keys outweighs the small advantages to be gained by learning many different fingerings. The seven double notes in the octave may invariably be fingered

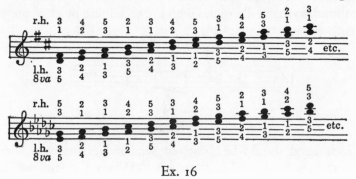

Ex. 16

$\frac{3\text{-}4\text{-}5}{1\text{-}2\text{-}3}$ $\frac{2\text{-}3\text{-}4\text{-}5}{1\text{-}1\text{-}2\text{-}3}$, the only problem being to determine where the initial double note of each scale begins in this series. As a help, the student should remember that, for either hand, scales with white tonics begin with the thumb on the tonic, those with black tonics begin so that the thumb will fall on a white key at the beginning of both the $\frac{3\text{-}4\text{-}5}{1\text{-}2\text{-}3}$ and the $\frac{2\text{-}3\text{-}4\text{-}5}{1\text{-}1\text{-}2\text{-}3}$ groups. Thus, the D major and E-flat natural-minor scales will be played as in Ex. 16.

Fingerings may also be recommended here for certain other double-note scales that give trouble. In Ex. 17 the chromatic scale in minor thirds is fingered so as to take advantage of the

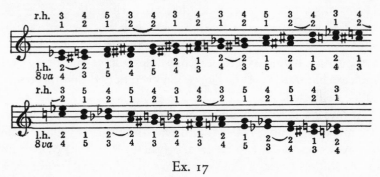

Ex. 17

slide from a black to a white key. It will be noted that the slide occurs only on the second finger and only from a black key that precedes two white keys. The scales in sixths may be fingered similarly to those in thirds, with $\frac{4\text{-}5}{2\text{-}3}$ always becoming $\frac{4\text{-}5}{1\text{-}2}$. The

Ex. 18

chromatic scale in major sixths, in which the slide cannot be used, may be played as in Ex. 18, both up and down, by those who can manage the stretches.

Other useful drills that have direct application in much music include all scales and arpeggios, played hands together an octave apart; trills in double notes, fingered $\frac{3\text{-}4}{1\text{-}2}$ and $\frac{4\text{-}5}{2\text{-}3}$ and played like Exs. 7 and 8; chromatic scales (for which the old fingering, using 1-3 and 1-2-3, usually proves to be safer than the fleeter but irregular sequence of 1-2-3-4, 1-2-3, 1-2-3-4, 1-2-3, 1-3, and so forth); arpeggios on diminished and dominant seventh chords; and all scales and arpeggios played in octaves, hands together. The student must understand that all such drills need to be practiced in the various rhythms that will be encountered in actual music. Playing in rhythms has the further advantage of keeping the hands exactly together. Groupings in threes and fours are naturally most common, but even dotted rhythms ought not be neglected.

Always good is the familiar instruction to set the metronome at a moderate tempo (60-80) and play the drill one octave, one note to a beat, once; two octaves, two notes to a beat, twice; and so on, adding notes to the beat even after the extreme range is reached. Scales are often smoothed out by playing them in fives, sixes (a pair of triplets), sevens (every tonic accented), and eights (a pair of fours). Frequently I recommend experiments with extreme speeds to my students as a means of eliminating waste motion. These are the speeds they are asked to try for:

> Scales, 7 notes to a beat of 120, 5 or 6 octaves
> Arpeggios, 12 notes to a beat of 60, 4 octaves
> Octave scales, 4 notes to a beat of 116, 3 or 4 octaves

These speeds may seem out of the question at first. But most students can approximate them as they learn to cut out superfluous tension, high finger raising, pounding, and other excesses to be discussed presently. Naturally, such skimming along the keys must be countered with a much greater percentage of slow, careful practice.

CREATING EXERCISES OUT OF ACTUAL SITUATIONS

There can be no question that the student resourceful and thorough enough to create the proper corrective exercise out of each technical deficiency that shows up in the actual music he plays will never need to bother with other exercises. Although we may rarely meet with resourcefulness and thoroughness to this ideal degree, it is my opinion that this still remains the ideal form of exercise in both efficiency and effectiveness, and one from which teachers and students can derive vastly more than

they ordinarily do. Shining evidence of this principle has come to me in numerous instances when students have gone at pieces presumably well beyond their technical levels, then surprised me by "rising to the occasion."

Recently a young lady begged to be allowed to study the now too-familiar Chopin *Polonaise* in A-flat major. Although this work, along with Debussy's *Clair de lune* and Lecuona's *Malaguena,* had been suffering inordinate exposure, and although she seemed to be much better prepared for the easier Chopin nocturnes, the project was approved because the factor of interest is so vital to learning. The results were astonishing and enlighten-

ing in more ways than one. They showed what a powerful moti-
vation interest can be, and, incidentally, how effectively the old
"play like me" instruction can operate (she had immediately
purchased the Rubinstein recording). They also showed that
careful, intelligent practice in the music itself, and that alone,
can produce technical achievements far in advance of the performance of routine drills.

Because the technical situations vary in the extreme from one
piece to the next, only a few general procedures for creating
exercises can be suggested here. (On pages 153 to 154 are illustrated ways to convert figures or "handfuls" of notes into double-
note exercises, along with specific examples.) The student must
be encouraged to analyze his own difficulties as soon as he is
interested in solving them. If an ascending scale in the left hand
trips up his fourth finger, a) what is wrong with the muscular
action or angle of approach, and b) what will correct it? This
attitude is not only desirable, but it is sometimes imperative.
Quirks, jerks, hitches, and skips have a way of marring a passage
in spite of the most dogged practice, if no effort is made to discover the cause. Try as he will, the conscientious teacher, who
has advised with every general principle that comes to mind,
may find that he cannot get at the trouble. The passage plays
smoothly enough for him. The cause, then, may very well lie in
the hand construction or the reflexes of the student, who must
discover the difficulty for himself, from the inside, so to speak.

When a technical impediment arises, the student should first
consider whether it is not merely a hesitation that will take care
of itself as the piece is played through again and again. If it is
not, then it should be isolated *along with its context* so that any
improvements can be incorporated into the performance without
further difficulties. Again, from Mr. Loesser:

"Eminently so. In fact, the very beginning of the troublesome
passage may be compromised by a disadvantageous hand position

necessitated by the previous passage. But smoothing a dubious passage into its context also helps remove the psychological tenderness created by lifting the passage out in the first place."

Out of this segment the student should try to invent, with the least possible alteration, a sort of perpetual-motion figure that will strengthen or correct the weak or faulty co-ordination. Very often this figure will be a rotary passage that reverses its direction, after moving forward, in order to start over again without a break. For instance, the troublesome right-hand thirds at the opening of Beethoven's Sonata in C, Op. 2, No. 3, may be "exercised" as in Ex. 19.

Ex. 19

Further help is gained, especially when one of the notes tends to be slurred over or skipped without sounding, by practicing the derived exercise in different rhythms from the source. Most commonly, triplets will be played in twos or vice versa. In this way, fingers falling on weak beats will get the exercise benefit of the changed accent. The principle of playing groups of notes in

Ex. 20

simultaneous clusters can have the same comprehension value that was noted above for scales and arpeggios. For instance, the bass in measures 15 and 16 of Chopin's *Revolutionary* Etude may be practiced as in Ex. 20.

ABOUT SITTING AND HAND POSITIONS

Both sensible and salutary is the current, widespread reaction
against those outworn, hard-and-fast "methods" of piano playing
that call for fixed, sometimes rigid, positions and uniform attacks
in all situations. In the first place, these methods fix the performer so primly and properly that we almost expect the piano
to come to him. Certainly, they do very little to help the performer adapt himself to the multiform requirements of the

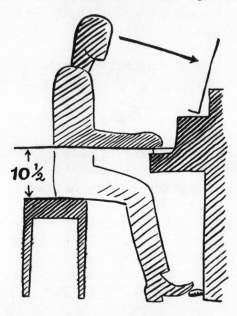

piano. If anything, they interfere with the constant adjustments
and extensions, both lateral and vertical, that must be made in
order to work in and out of the black and white keys with short
and long fingers. The use of a lowered wrist, with fingers neatly
rounded and knuckles held in, may recall pictures of the young
Mozart or resemble Iturbi's position as seen in the movies, but

that hardly means that it will be the ideal for all pianists or all music.

The real ideals of position are pliability, adaptability, and that sort of easy yet alert posture that comes half way between a rigid and a slumped position. The average student who is healthy and normally graceful needs but little instruction to fall into good habits of posture. Often when he attacks the piano awkwardly there are other factors responsible. The most common is the use of a bench that is too high or too low. Since the height of the piano itself varies considerably, the best measure is the distance from the surface of the keys (that is, the ivories) down to the compressed top of the bench. About ten inches is normal. Very short persons or persons with short arms may prefer to lessen that distance by as much as an inch. Sitting too low, which is perhaps the worse of the two evils, constrains the finger action by raising the wrists; sitting too high constrains the wrist action by lowering the wrists. Another factor affecting position is bad eyesight, which often causes the performer to edge closer and closer to the piano in order to read his music. The adjustable music rack on most grand pianos usually relieves this problem.

A few recommendations regarding position will suffice here, along with the reminder that individual differences may justify surprising variations. It is best to sit only on the front half of the bench; covering the whole bench induces slumping. The edge of the knees should be not more than an inch or two under the keyboard. In this position, which will seem far out to some, the body is alert for action, both rhythmic and athletic. Moreover, the arms and shoulders have full freedom and the wrist action is not cramped. The balls of the feet should rest on the "balls" of the outer pedals, ready to pedal at a moment's notice. Intertwining the feet around the bench legs not only interferes with ready pedaling, but causes the back to slump and thus lessens endurance in long practice. In fact, the legs, arms, and back work

somewhat as a unit. Their improper alignment leads to early
fatigue and faulty wrist action, as is suggested in the accompany-
ing diagram. The performance of octaves, in particular, requires
that the performer be firmly planted.

The elbows should be several inches out from the body.
Putting them out compensates in part for the short fifth finger.
Pressing them against the body constrains the shoulder, arm,
and wrist action. The elbow tips will usually be on a horizontal
level with the finger tips if the performer is sitting at the right
height. The middle of the keyboard comes between e′ and f′ but
most players prefer to sit in front of (that is, with their nose on

a vertical line with) middle C or d′. Finger and wrist positions
vary with the type of technique, as discussed presently. The
student will profit by watching himself in a mirror now and then
as he plays, noting in particular the items just mentioned. For
that matter, the teacher, who is accustomed to giving all his
lessons from one viewpoint in the studio, will be surprised at
the new concept he may get of the student's playing position
by moving to the other side of him.

The player who leans far to the left or right to play passages
in the extreme ranges should bear in mind that he is upsetting
the support for his aim. He is taxing himself somewhat as a

gunner would who attempts to shoot on the run. Furthermore, by moving his arms and body as a single unit he sacrifices a desirable freedom at the shoulders. Playing scales in contrary motion from the center to the extreme ends of the keyboard helps to correct this fault when it is a fault.

THE FOUR PLAYING MECHANISMS

It is common knowledge that all playing is done by the finger working from the knuckle at its base, the hand from the

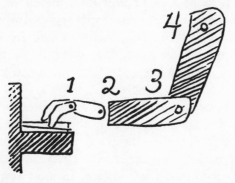

wrist, the forearm from the elbow, and the upper arm from the shoulder. The useful application of this knowledge through further deductions is not so common. First, some general principles may be stated. These four mechanisms are used separately or in various combinations. So that any one of them may be specified where needed or avoided where not desired, the student should first learn to play each mechanism by itself. He may do this merely by playing the five fingers in succession, up and down, practicing each mechanism in turn.

If he understands how each mechanism is based on the leverage principle he will be able to control it more intelligently. Thus, the key is the object of the force exerted by the lever; the playing mechanism (finger, hand, forearm, or upper arm) is the lever;

the joint (knuckle, wrist, elbow, or shoulder) is the fulcrum; and the section remaining above the joint in use (hand, forearm, upper arm, or the body itself) provides the stationary support for the fulcrum as well as the base for the muscle that connects with and propels the lever.

This means that when the fingers alone are playing, the hand and arm are immobile; when the hand alone plays, it plays as a one-piece unit from the wrist to the finger tips, there being no "give" in the fingers or motion in the arm; when the forearm alone plays, it forms a single unit from the elbow to the finger tips, and the upper arm remains stationary; and when the upper arm alone plays, it forms one unbroken unit from shoulder to finger tips. In each instance, too, there is no movement or "break" at any of the joints except the one on which the particular playing mechanism hinges.

When each mechanism is played alone throughout the range or orbit that the joint permits, only the fingers can play legato. In fact, the fingers are then the primary means of playing legato, the hands of playing staccato, and the forearm and upper arm of playing heavy octaves and chords. In most piano music the fingers and hand do the lion's share of the playing, but it is rare when the others do not contribute, at least in combination with the former. For instance, among the niceties of performance required by the Mozart style, the precise distinction between legato and staccato is largely accomplished by fingers and hand, whereas the familiar, stepwise, two-note slurs are best initiated, and the sudden accents in the course of more rapid passage work are best achieved, by the entire arm worked in one piece, with the next tone(s) played by finger action alone.

These latter, supplementary uses of the forearm and upper arm are made possible by the important fact that only these mechanisms can roll sideways as well as move in a vertical axis from their respective joints. One may also note that all the mechanisms are able to move on a lateral as well as a vertical axis and that the fingers can even push forward by virtue of separate finger joints. Similar forward thrusts can also be made by the other three mechanisms when they are variously combined. Indeed, by combining all four mechanisms in various ways, there is no direction in which force cannot be exerted. Note, for instance, the peculiar rotary motions from shoulder to finger tips that are required for continued, rapid repeated notes, with the fingers sweeping down the key in the order 3-2-1 or 4-3-2-1. (The nature of this movement, incidentally, tends to make repetition more successful when fingered toward rather than away from the thumb. For example, 3-2 is usually better than 2-3.)

Besides the idea of leverage one other mechanical relationship must be understood by the player. This concerns the inverse ratio of speed to power. Much faulty playing and harsh sound can be spared by the constant reminder that an increase in speed must mean a sacrifice in power, and vice versa. The analogy of the automobile's standard or old-type gearshift with overdrive is illuminating within limits. We use low or first gear (the upper arm) when maximum power rather than smooth speed is the first consideration. We use second gear (the forearm) when we still need extra power, but with a little more speed. We use third gear (the hand) when we want enough driving speed, though still with a degree of power available. And finally, we use top gear or overdrive (the fingers) for that substantial part of the driving where maximum, smooth speed and not power is the prime consideration. Pianists need power mainly for loudness. Perhaps the main deduction to be made from this principle is the fact that too much power can be a nuisance. For *utmost efficiency* we must *use the least powerful mechanism that will answer the need*. When we are driving on the open highway we do not use low or second gear because *a)* that would be a waste of power

(power is a vital factor in piano endurance) and *b*) that would delimit the speed. Both objections concern serious technical faults to be found in the playing of many earnest, hard-working students. They are further considered in the individual discussions of the four playing mechanisms that follow.

THE USE OF THE FINGERS

The big problem in teaching the use of the fingers is to get them actually into use. Once this is achieved, the matters of correct stroke and the special movement of the thumb may or may not have to be considered, depending upon the natural aptitudes of the student. Without instruction to the contrary most students (as well as most pianists who are badly out of practice) do their playing by impulses from the arm, the fingers moving just enough so that the whole hand does not strike at once. This kind of playing is evident in a very common jogging or bouncing motion of the hand and arm that results in reduced speed and control. The speed, in fact, is limited to that of the arm jogging!

Ignorance of finger action and laziness partly account for this fault. Also responsible are misguided efforts to exploit the weight of the arm. The familar weight-of-the-arm prescription is very misleading. Obviously, to rest the arm's full weight or, as the alternative expression goes, to "relax completely" merely results in utter limpness and a collapse of the leverage principle. In piano playing the popular remark about gravity must be reversed: what goes down must come up. The more weight that is dropped the more that must be lifted. In short, we are back to the principle that advises the use of only as large a mechanism (for which, read "only as much weight") as the music requires at any one time. The dropping of too much weight means unnecessary effort quite as much as a too rigid or tense support of unused weight means unnecessary effort. In slow music, the use of arm weight, rested upon a sufficiently braced finger, is an ideal means of producing a full, rounded, yet unforced tone because there is ample time to draw so heavy a mechanism back up again. But as the speed increases, the pianist who tries to maintain the same weight will merely wear himself down by exerting more and more effort until he is stopped, in any case, by his physical limitations.

Another cause of arm jogging is the desire to play louder and sound bigger than the fingers alone will permit. This desire to play loud and sound big is a matter of taste if not inexperience. It has been widely condemned but perhaps it is indicative of artistic trends in these tempestuous times. Personally, I hope not. I hope that the piano is not becoming more and more of a percussion instrument at the expense of its fine capabilities for lyricism and poetry, and at the expense of a very precious element in art—gentleness. However that may be, when the volume demanded is too great for the fingers, the other mechanisms involuntarily come into play. The other mechanisms are bigger and more powerful and hence the speed is curtailed, as just explained. The lack of control comes both with the use of bulkier mechanisms and with their nondescript combination in a most exasperating kind of snakelike motion. Without a firm support or base for his finger action, the pianist is in the position of a gardener who tries to weed with a rubber-handled hoe.

To correct this fault the student may try playing scales in one hand while he endeavors to keep the forearm still by holding it just above the wrist with his free hand. He may also try the old stunt of balancing a penny on the back or "small" of each wrist while playing scales with both hands. The fatigue that comes from picking up the pennies a good many times acts like a sort of sulphur-and-molasses curative. A third help is the exaggerated raising of the fingers so that each one strikes like a little metallic hammer and pops back the instant it is released, as far as the knuckle permits. However, all three methods must be used as emergency remedies only. They impose excess tension on the base (wrist or forearm), hence could lead to severe tightness. Too few pianists realize that such tightness is often a result of faulty finger action. Of course, with too tight a wrist there is no "universal joint" by which the arm can adapt to bumps in its "road"—that is, the ups and downs of black- and white-key positions and of short and long fingers.

Unfortunately, high finger raising still survives as the standard mode of playing among far too many pianists, a mode that stems from Czerny and his contemporaries. In a valuable study called *The Riddle of the Pianist's Finger* (listed under Source References), Arnold Schultz concludes that the finger should be worked primarily by the small muscles of the hand; that is, the muscles that connect its first phalanx to the underside of the hand rather than the forearm muscles and their connecting tendons, which may be seen and felt both on the topside of the hand and the underside of the wrist. The forearm muscles and their tendons excel only in force, but have marked disadvantages in speed, control, and their binding effect on the wrist. When the small muscles are used, any finger raising above the keys becomes a waste of time and energy. But this fact does not mean the fingers should not be worked with conscious pressure and effort. Very popular in recent years has been the opposite idea of "dripping" the fingers effortlessly into the keys, from a hand suspended limply by the wrist and rolled by arm rotation. This fluent method, easiest for players with long, slim fingers, is wonderfully effective in rapid, velvety, legato, Chopinesque passages. But it is only one style of playing. It certainly does not answer for the neat articulation required in much other passage work. By all means, the use of the fingers must not become a lost art!

The same Mr. Schultz further concludes that the finger stroke, if it is to attain its maximum efficiency, will be forward as well as downward. That is, the finger will push "through" its two joints. This stroke is consistent with the present-day preference for flatter fingers. Also, it comes as a boon to those pianists who happen to have finger joints that "break" or cave in when the finger presses into the keys. A more perpendicular stroke may even induce the breaking at the joints, especially if the finger-nail is too long, thus causing the finger to skid into a flatter position with its tip turned up like a boat prow. This fact and the nuisance of clicking sounds are, incidentally, reasons enough why all pianists must file (never bite or cut!) their nails regularly, fashionable young ladies included. In any case, there are certain pianists who cannot use the perpendicular stroke because their nails cannot be trimmed above the finger tips without causing soreness.

Actually, the tightly rounded finger that was formerly pre-scribed is not only unnatural, it is impractical. If it follows through the circular arc that it describes, as it must if its position is to be maintained, then it tends to strike the key at an inward tangent, whereas a flatter finger can achieve a direct stroke. The tangential stroke reduces the finger's force substantially. Furthermore, a too-rounded finger constrains the hand action and lessens the stretch. To determine just how rounded his fingers should be, the student needs only observe their position when his arms are hanging limply at his sides.

The thumb action obviously differs from that of the other fingers, to which it is in a sense opposed. It has a freer orbit and moves easiest sideways rather than up and down. If we had twenty vertical-axis fingers on a hand we could probably play them in succession as rapidly as we can play a twenty-tone glis-sando. But with only five fingers, one of which (the thumb) does only the shifting and another of which (the fifth) plays only the final notes, we seem to encounter a sort of supersonic barrier to unlimited speed. I say "seem" because in actuality the thumb does not have to hold back the other fingers. The reason it does so may very well be that too much is made of its special type of movement.

Take, for example, the old rule, widely taught in scale playing, that says the thumb must "snap" ahead, as if released from a slingshot, to the next note it will play the very instant it is succeeded by the second finger. This brisk act looks admirable when the scale is played slowly and imparts much the same pleasurable sense of robust, muscular vigor that we get from doing our "daily dozen" each morning. It can even help the hand to avoid the quick hoisting of the wrist at the moment the thumb passes under, a fault that produces severe humps in the scale. Yet, curiously, the faster the scale is played the more this snap shift becomes an impediment to be unlearned rather than an aid. Snapping the thumb under the hand while the other fingers are in motion is not a natural act. It seems to require the second finger to serve as a pivot. The momentary delay thus entailed stands out increasingly as the speed increases.

Note that this rule about the thumb action is applied only when the hand plays away from the thumb side or the center of the piano. Yet, again curiously, most pianists agree that the hand plays easier, smoother, and faster when it returns to the center. Why do we not apply the same rule on the return, posting the thumb ahead each time it is released? The answer seems to be in the fact that the student who is not taught to snap his thumb under his hand seldom has any trouble with it. He will probably do best if he is told merely to play the scale away from the center of the piano as if the hand were pulled along a lateral track by the elbow, provided this instruction is not interpreted as prohibiting compensatory play at the wrist joint, thus causing formal stiffness. Then the thumb will trail along the edge of the keys and have no difficulty taking its place, in its proper turn, with the other fingers. Furthermore, the pull from the elbow tends to induce the forward finger stroke recommended above. The same position may be used on the return, with the elbow pushing instead of pulling.

In the discussion of the four mechanisms the chief function of the fingers was stated to be legato playing. However, they are capable of much more. In fact they can play everything from overlapping tones to crisp staccatos (except in wide skips or passages where the same finger repeats). The overlapping can be done only at slow to moderate tempos. But the staccatos, produced by popping each finger back at the knuckle as it releases the key, can be played, in fact are best played, very rapidly and often serve for elflike passages that are beyond the speed that the hand and wrist can manage.

Overlapping, semilegato (or *portato*, often wrongly called *portamento*), and staccato can be controlled by deliberate regulation of the interval between the release of one key and the depression of the next. Otherwise, for subtle variations in the degree of legato this deliberate regulation becomes too fussy a task. The teacher can often get the desired results much more readily and successfully by simply asking the student to "hug" closer and closer to the keys, using less and less finger movement, when he wants to increase the degree of legato. As always, the student will be greatly helped by first hearing and seeing what is wanted.

While on the subject of legato, mention should be made of two other difficulties. One is the plodding or choppy effect that seems to come in certain passages in spite of the most careful finger legato. It shows up particularly in the even eighth- or sixteenth-note passages that are so common in music of moderate tempo by Bach. The best antidote for this is to place more emphasis on the natural rhythmic groupings, giving just that degree of nuance within the groups that the character of the music permits. The nuance or, for that matter, any gradual change of volume, and the clear rhythmic organization combine to give a distinct illusion of legato over and above that achieved by the fingers. Mr. Loesser calls attention to the "synthetic nature" of all legato on the piano:

> "A true legato consists of making two or more successive tones with one impulse (bow, breath, and so on). Such a thing is impossible on a keyboard instrument, and can only be simulated."

The other difficulty occurs in trying to make two successive octaves or other double notes sound legato when one of the fingers has to be repeated. If both fingers try to play legato at once, the result is that neither one does. The remedy is to lift off the repeated finger before the other finger moves. That leaves one finger to be played legato (it is better if this can be the finger for the upper note), creating the illusion that both notes have been approached legato.

THE USE OF THE HAND

The hand, too, is a vehicle for both staccato and legato. If the reader wonders why so much importance is attached to a thorough command of legato and staccato, he must remind himself that in essence these cover everything that can be done by way of varied attack and release at the piano. The violinist can choose from an extraordinary variety of bowings (not to mention pizzicato), he can swell or diminish the tone at will, and he can qualify the tone by differing degrees of vibrato and sensitive intonation. The pianist, on the other hand, can control but two things: the volume of the tone at the instant of attack and the duration of the tone while it lasts. That is all. On these two controls he must depend for everything that constitutes style and interpretation in piano music.

The function of the hand is the converse of the function of the fingers. The chief duty of the hand is to play staccato, but it can be a major agent in legato playing when it is flexibly combined with the finger action. Among the staccato uses for the hand are the playing of octaves and other double notes, of chords within comfortable reach, and of all single notes, whether separate or grouped, that are not too fast for the wrist action. The essential point in playing crisp staccatos is to get off the key in a hurry, as if it were a hot coal that had been touched. As a teacher once instructed me, "When you pay a short visit, what matters is not how soon you get there but how soon you leave." Anything that delays the release will spoil the crispness of the staccato. In other words, if the finger joints "break" so that the hand does not play in one piece from wrist to finger tips, or if the forearm jogs along without providing the firm, unyielding support necessary to the wrist fulcrum, the finger will drag along the key before it actually releases.

Depending on the context, there are two preferred means of leaving the key instantly. One is to start from above the key, drop the hand on a firm finger tip, and rebound from the wrist. This is used to play a series of staccato notes in succession. A common fault occurs in this method when the student timidly drops his finger to the key level and hesitates an instant to find the place—with, of course, the complete loss of a rebound.

The other means of release is necessary wherever the hand must start from the keyboard rather than above, as at the end of a legato phrase or slur, thus making the rebound impossible. It is needed only for one staccato at a time, since, for any other staccatos that may follow, the hand will immediately be in position to rebound once more. To play this kind of staccato the hand must draw back sharply at the wrist (taking care not to grow tense in mid-air); in fact, it must seem to strike the note by drawing back. Again, if the student questions the value of this much detail he must be assured that these methods of release are among the most essential technical means for putting life and sparkle into his playing. They are indispensable, for example, to the spirited performance of most quick music by Haydn, Mozart, and Beethoven.

Successful octaves depend a great deal on the stretch and the structure of the hand. Stretch is determined as much by the width of the webs between the fingers as by the length of the fingers themselves. Pianists can often manage one kind of stretch and not another, as may be realized when attempting such differently constructed chords as those in Ex. 21. Of course, there are stretches in music that give trouble to almost all pianists; but

Ex. 21

the performer who cannot reach a minor tenth from a black to a white key (and cannot afford the smaller, custom-built keyboard used by Josef Hofmann) must expect to alter the notes of the larger chords or "break" them by starting before the beat. Players with a narrow stretch find that the effort to reach an octave inhibits or tightens the wrist action to the point where the octaves must be played by the forearm working in one piece with the hand and fingers.

To be sure, there are always a few staunch advocates of the forearm method of playing octaves, but most pianists prefer to use their hands, with the forearm serving as an immobile base. Speed and power can meet halfway if the full arm is used to supply the initial impetus for each rhythmic group of three or four octaves. It can do this either by dropping at the wrist or thrusting forward and up at the wrist, then gradually returning to its former position during the remaining octaves of the group.

To get the feel of correct wrist action the student may start by exaggerating the vertical movement of his hand throughout the complete range of the wrist joint. Thereafter, he will discover that the secret of rapid, fluent octaves, as, indeed, of all physical effort, is minimum motion. All key slap must be eliminated in efficient octave playing. Often helpful, if the stretch permits, are a slightly arched hand and an elevated wrist, with firm fingers working in a single unit with the hand.

Octaves on black keys are normally played with the thumb and fourth finger, so as to avoid the in-and-out motion that the black and white keys otherwise cause and to enable the playing of legato chromatic octaves. This principle presupposes that the white octaves will be played by the thumb and fifth finger at least as far in as the edge of the black keys. Please note that when the pianist strains too hard to reach octaves with his third or fourth finger, the results will be exactly what he means to avoid: hardness, nonlegato, and clumsiness.

The hand may work in conjunction with but independently of the fingers to produce a very pliant legato and a secure grasp of the keys. To achieve this, the student must learn to move the fingers and hand laterally at the knuckles and wrist at least as much as he moves them vertically. The process is an art in itself and one that affords the pianist a pleasurable and confident sense of being in control. The process is also one that is easier seen and felt than described because it seems to come from within the hand. The pianist must think of fitting right into the varied molds formed by the myriad positions among the black and white keys. He must feel that he is reaching forward and to either side, in a most flexible, supple manner, to play whatever lies within range without budging the forearm. This approach to the keyboard is especially appropriate in Bach's music when it becomes necessary for one hand to maintain the contrapuntal integrity of two or more expressive, legato lines.

THE USE OF THE FOREARM AND THE UPPER ARM

Employed in single, one-piece units, the forearm and upper arm can perform heavier chords and octaves with that strength needed, for example, in the popular concertos by Liszt, Tschaikowsky, and Rachmaninoff. The forearm, being faster and better controlled, is naturally used more often in this way than the upper arm. Only infrequently does either unit strike from the full height to which its joint (elbow or shoulder) permits it to be raised. Yet, I recall that just such a procedure was almost a mannerism with Paderewski. That rare artist, whose technique alone would not rank him among the world's greatest virtuosos, did have a way of raising his arm and hand high above his head so that he could crash it down in a single unit from the shoulder, striking his chord with uncanny accuracy and all the while fixing his eyes in a cold stare toward the audience. In such attacks the wrist must remain locked, for a collapse here only dissipates the force of the attack. (Recall the rubber-handled hoe.) Yet, tempo permitting, the wrist must yield, up or down, enough to absorb the shock, like a resilient buffer. To avoid sounding and looking brittle requires some vertical give and take at the wrist much as down-up violin bowing requires lateral wrist play.

As for the various combination touches, their misuses must be known in order to profit from their good uses. We have already seen how the arm can hamper hand or finger action by jogging along and not providing a firm base against which these lighter "levers" can react. And there are those excessive arm rotations that show up mostly in slow, expressive playing, including undulating wrists and elbows like wing tips! Their doubtful use to "free" the arm or stimulate rhythmic flow is surely canceled by their distracting, sentimental appearance to the audience.

But we have also seen how helpful the upper arm in particular can be. It can initiate each slur, grouping, or handful of notes played by fingers or wrist, shifting the hand from one to the next. It can precipitate a series of "free" rebounds, like dropping a rubber ball; or follow through a cascade of notes, like swinging a golf club. And it can co-operate well with the other mechanisms in rotary motions, such as that noted for rapid repeated notes. To these useful combination movements may be added others even more familiar. One is the rotation of the forearm (at the radio-ulnar joints) to play a tremolo, usually aided by finger action. The value of this rotation is known to lessen with increased volume and with smaller intervals, most trills being best played with fingers alone. Another is rotation at the shoulder and wrist to play broken chords, as at both ends of a white-key arpeggio, or to extend the hand position either way. This motion compensates for the short thumb and fifth finger and eases the burden of tiring circular passages. But it is not a panacea for all difficulties. Thus, it is misapplied when it is used too vigorously and in place of all finger action; or when the passage is not genuinely circular, as at the end of Chopin's *Fantaisie Impromptu;* or when the fingers alone can achieve better control, as at the start of the "Moonlight Sonata."

Of course, all rotary motion suffers if the posture is slumped. Then the shoulders are bound and their use is even overlooked.

TOUCH AND TONE—FACT AND FANCY

Touch, tone, and pedaling, which are the remaining topics to be discussed under the general heading of Technique, might also have been included under musicianship, for they are skills that rarely reach perfection among unmusical performers. Here I insert a valued comment supplied by the eminent American composer and pianist Arthur Shepherd, who argues for an approach to these problems that is almost entirely by way of the musical senses:

"I have never been greatly interested in *theories* of piano technique. The *mechanics* of the thing I find rather boresome. To 'lift or not to lift,' to 'rotate or not to rotate'—why labor such banal problems?

"This brings me to a note out of my own experience. I am a firm believer in the *empirical* approach. Piano playing, I believe, becomes a subtle, sensitive interplay of psycho-physical attributes. Touch, tone, tactility are all governed by a divining *ear*. Without the interplay of these factors or in the absence thereof, the piano is, I feel, the *worst* of all instruments.

"In my piano playing days I discovered over and over again that the way through a technical problem was by *ear*!

"Oh, I don't mean to say that a conscious physical analysis is not incidentally to be reckoned with, but I do mean to say that the controlling and directing ear or aural faculty is too often forgotten, undeveloped, or left out of account.

"How many pianists, do you suppose, have the well developed faculty of *hearing* sensitively and objectively what they are playing? With singers, the question is even more crucial.

"Nowadays, in our mechanistic-ridden life we can and do fall back on disc and tape recordings to reveal the result of our doings. How much more important is the ability to co-ordinate our faculties on the basis of sound musicianship without exteriorizing the mechanics or spoiling the game by a priori theorizing?"

A great deal has been written and said about touch, tone, and pedaling, but only a little need be stated here, chiefly to right certain misconceptions.

As is generally known by now, the word *touch,* which is intimately bound up with the word *tone,* is something of a misnomer. The fact has been conclusively established that the style of striking the key cannot affect the timbre that results, whether the striking agent be a brick, a kitten's paw, or a human finger. (Mr. Loesser observes, in this connection, that he likes to show how the right hand of Chopin's familiar Nocturne in E-flat major can be made to sound at least as well with a pencil, preferably one provided with a noiseless eraser, as with the naked finger.) Once the hammer strikes for a fraction of a second it simply has no further contact with the string. Consequently, one hardly need add that common statements like "she has a lovely touch," and impressive acts like the effort to produce a vibrato after the key is struck, represent basic misconceptions.

What, then, produces the *illusion* of touch or the sense of tone production? Mostly one thing, and that is the relative volume or weight of the tone. By *relative* I mean the volume of one tone as compared with any other tones being sounded. For example, play the lyrical chord line that announces the main theme in the first movement of the Schumann Concerto, giving equal weight to all tones. The result will be dull and nondescript. Now play the same passage with each top chord tone appropriately emphasized and an illusion of "touch" results. I may seem to oversimplify, yet might even add that to produce the renowned "singing tone" of Hofmann and others mainly means *hearing that each tone of a melodic line sounds over the accompaniment and right into the next tone,* especially each long-lasting tone.

The degree to which the melody tone should be brought out in chords naturally varies widely with the expressive intent of the music. However, inexperienced pianists commonly understate this tone by a considerable amount. They do not realize how clearly the tone can be projected before it sounds like forcing or even pounding. Pounding rarely occurs when tones are played according to their relative importance, assuming the pedaling is clear and the instrument's capacity is not exceeded.

To practice this tone production the student may distribute an eight-tone chord between his two hands and endeavor to bring out each tone in turn. His first step will be to extend the particular finger and play the desired tone slightly in advance of the others. When the teacher can guess which tone he means to bring out, the student is on the right track. Playing one hand louder than the other is ordinarily learned without difficulty. In strongly metrical music, however, the student may find that he is successful only in subordinating the quieter hand on the off-beats—that he is producing no difference where the difference matters most, on the accented beats that the hands play together.

Four other factors also influence the production of the tone.

One of these is certainly the degree of legato, discussed earlier. Another is the use of the pedals, to be discussed presently. A third is any attendant noise element. And a fourth, the most important, is control of the key descent.

Noise may result, of course, from vibrations in the room or action squeaks. Or it may result from slapping on the key surface, which hints at inefficient attacks that must be remedied.

Control of the key descent is possible only in slow music, but that is where tone production matters the most. In effect, to control the key descent one must start *on*, not above, the key and stick right with it down to the bottom or key bed. At the same time he must slightly but constantly increase the speed of attack as the key descends in order to maintain contact with it and control over it. We encounter the same principle if we push a little boy in his coaster wagon. If we give just one abrupt shove, the wagon leaves us immediately and is out of our control. If, on the other hand, we begin in contact with it so that we gradually push faster, we continue to keep the wagon in control. The significance of this procedure is that by keeping in contact with the key during its descent we have exact control over the volume that will result. However, as Mr. Loesser effectively illustrates, any effort to maintain the contact after the tone is sounded merely taxes the student's "peace of mind and muscle":

> "Students are constantly falling into the same illusion that afflicts telegraphers' apprentices: when the telegraph key makes its contact a buzz is heard; the young operator has the feeling that he is making the sound and presses hard. The 'firmness of contact' that occurs is regarded as a very bad habit, leading to cramp and fatigue. The manuals on telegraphy warn against it very explicitly. Likewise, 'firmness of contact' is to be avoided on the piano."

Now, the quality of a piano tone does change from "cloudy" to "bright" as it gets louder (with more high partials). Though this is a fixed change it matters much in sensitive nuance. In any case, as the pianist gains increasing mastery of his skills, the matter of touch and tone becomes less and less a question of technique. The qualities of gentleness or stridence or thinness or fullness that we come to associate with particular artists of experience represent, primarily, differences of personality and temperament.

DO YOU HEAR WHAT YOU PEDAL?

There is a reason why pedaling is a much neglected subject in piano study, a subject only cursorily treated by the teacher

and seldom noticed by the student. Pedaling is a highly sensitive, almost nervous, art, dependent entirely on the ear of the performer. Students often fail to hear their pedaling for the reason that hearing seems to be the least pressing among the many responsibilities that they must bear in mind. Sometimes they pedal merely to hide a multitude of sins, as the expression goes.

Editorial suggestions for pedaling are bound to be inadequate and misleading because good pedaling is a matter of the performance at any one moment—of the instrument, the location, and the mood of the player; and because good pedaling involves many more movements and half movements and variations in timing than could possibly be indicated by an editor. Faithful adherence to the editorial markings for the pedal will be practiced only by unmusical performers and in any case must lead to many bad sounds.

Pedaling depends, of course, on style and color. The damper pedal, whose misuse is apparent in the popular designation "loud" pedal, governs sonority. When it is pressed down, it enriches the tone by reinforcing its overtones—that is, by allowing the other strings in tune with its overtones to vibrate sympathetically. The whole instrument seems to resonate. When the pedal is let up, the tone is correspondingly deadened. The kind of sonorities appropriate for Bach, Mozart, Liszt, and Debussy will differ widely (as illustrated more specifically on page 154). In this matter of styles the teacher can be of real help. Otherwise, beyond showing the how of "syncopated pedaling" his best help can be to remind and re-remind the student to hear what he plays.

Syncopated pedaling means the continuous, overlapping sort in which the foot lifts exactly as each new harmony is played, pressing down again to retain that harmony before the fingers release and while the next harmony is being approached. The procedure looks simple but it is still largely a matter for the ear. Low tones in broken chords are hard to catch in the pedal. Sometimes a low tone can be caught by the middle (or sostenuto) pedal, though the use of this pedal to retain only certain tones is seldom effective except in recent music where composers such as Debussy have deliberately allowed time for its operation. (Unfortunately, the middle pedal can be counted on to function properly only in the best grand pianos.) Otherwise, the low tone must be held while the upper tones change harmonies. Then the ear must decide how much can be blurred, how much can be taken care of by "half pedals" (made possible by the fact that the higher vibrations die out more quickly), and how much must be lost. Blurring is an art, too.

"Indeed it is," Mr. Loesser adds. "For instance, a single unchanged harmony can endure a certain amount of impurity without unpleasantness; but any confusion of harmonies intended to be different is annoying. The amount of dissonance involved is not in itself the determining factor. Another thing: the psychological effect of the blur is determined by the amount of time it is given to sink into the mind. A blur rapidly obliterated is hardly interpreted as such, but rather as smoothness or legato. But relative loudness also affects the endurability of a blur. Play a few notes softly with the pedal down, and let them die away to a *pianissimo*. There will be no harmonic impurity, merely a 'color' effect. Now play some unrelated chords *forte* without changing the pedal. The criticism 'too much pedal' must be carefully understood; usually it means 'not enough pedals.' "

Blurring is out of place in Mozart but absolutely necessary in Debussy and often very effective in Chopin. In chromatic, contrapuntal, or other music with kaleidoscopic, fluctuating harmonies, the pedal usually has to be applied in a tentative, fleeting manner. All too few pianists realize that inappropriate blurring will produce the illusion of a harsh touch quite, indeed, as will the opposite fault of unsuccessful finger legato.

With regard to the soft pedal, the problem is naturally somewhat less since this pedal does not need to be changed as the harmony changes. Its purpose is to lessen the volume and the richness of the tone, which purpose is achieved with better effect on a grand piano, where one or two of the unison strings are eliminated so as to leave but *due corde* or *una corda*, than on the upright, where the hammer stroke is merely shortened. The soft pedal is first of all important as a color device, especially in Romantic and Impressionistic music. It is also of great practical value in producing softer playing than the technique of the pianist can otherwise produce. But purists sometimes object to this use of the soft pedal, saying that loud and soft playing, however delicate the latter, must always be under muscular control.

III. Practice

I T SEEMS to me that the most important mission of the piano teacher is to guide the practice toward the day when the student can become his own teacher. Working himself out of a job, as it were, the teacher should help the student meet his

pianistic challenges until eventually the student makes himself independent of formal teaching. Nor should the "eventually" go on too long. Just as some grown children can never quite free themselves of their emotional dependence on their parents, so some grown students can never quite trust themselves to forge ahead without instruction. If they leave one teacher they must move on to another. (A more aggravated form of this anomaly is the student who insists that he must continue lessons in order to be made to practice, whether out of respect for the financial investment or fear of the teacher's displeasure.) The best thing in the world for such students, who are often very advanced in their skills and experience, is the working up and presentation of a recital entirely on their own, come what may.

Now, all this is not to belittle the absolute necessity of the teacher in the training of the pianist; nor to underestimate the time this training takes, or the need for meticulous supervision, or even the value of outside criticism throughout one's musical career. The purpose here is to suggest a basic line of procedure in our teaching: help the student to help himself. Certainly, like the parent with the child, the teacher himself can be responsible for the student's dependence. He can, for example, write in the student's fingering, demonstrate his rhythms (only too often teaching them by rote), or dictate his own interpretation, until it is he and not the student who learns the piece! The student who is placed more on his own will err and he will show bad taste, of course. But that is where the teacher should figure. From the very start, the teacher should be the good counselor who questions the fingering, or the rhythm, or the interpretation that the student brings in; and who suggests the further possibilities from which the student chooses. Only in this way will the student develop the creative imagination, the self-criticism, and the confidence that he must have when he is ready to carry on alone. And only in this way will the student become a complete musical personality in his own right, with the courage and independent judgment to give full expression to his own musical feelings. (Naturally, this *laissez-faire* policy must not be construed as an excuse for the unimaginative teacher who merely listens in blank silence, concluding the lesson with comments that are neither constructive nor specific, such as, "Not so good;

try harder next time." That sort of teacher may play well but he has not learned to teach.)

We have a first clue, now, as to how the student should practice. He must expect to lead himself with the teacher's guidance, but *not be led by the hand*. Next comes the very important question, What should he practice? For a preliminary answer we may recall the basic principle introduced with the discussion of technique: The student should practice exactly what he wants to learn and—if the practice is to attain maximum efficiency—*only* what he wants to learn. Put differently, he should examine his goal and let the obstacles that keep him from it be what he practices.

This principle is one of those apparent truisms that come home with increasing force as more and more of their ramifications are appreciated. The student wants to learn to play the piano. To do this he must learn one piece after another until he has acquired the wealth of experiences that make the well-rounded performer. From the practice standpoint his main concern is how to learn a new piece, and that is what is demonstrated in some detail in the nine steps that make up our fifth chapter. Here are discussed the ideas that govern those steps, especially as regards fingering, counting, interpretation, efficiency, and memorizing.

FINGERING CAN MAKE OR BREAK A PIECE

There are three rudiments of piano playing that brook *absolutely no compromise of exactness* in practice. These are NOTES, FINGERING, and COUNTING. The student must be expected to take full responsibility for these rudiments once they have been explained, without the necessity for having them constantly policed at his lessons. Carelessness in their regard makes the conscientious teacher writhe, for he knows that any performance built on such a foundation has no more security than a house built with rotten lumber. The necessity for playing the correct notes is usually self-evident and rarely gives lasting trouble. The importance of precise, careful fingering and accurate counting, however, is not so clear to the student, who may continue to neglect them, with nearly fatal consequences to the music, until stringent remedial measures are taken. Unfortunately, the student who stems from inferior teaching almost invariably reveals carelessness and indifference in fingering and counting.

Our fingers are the means of contact between ourselves and

the piano. All that we study and practice so hard is finally put into effect by these fingers. Which ones to use in what situations is the problem. The choice is somewhat like finding the right tool for a particular job. A disadvantageous choice of fingers means inefficiency if not actual failure in speed, power, and control. The best leverage applied by any of the four mechanisms can be undone in this way. Thus, the choice of and adherence to a fingering on a keyboard instrument can make or break a piece. It can profoundly affect memorizing, stage poise, technical mastery, speed of learning, and general security at the piano. Only among stringed instruments does the matter of fingering assume equivalent proportions. In wind instruments it reduces itself to a relatively small number of clearly defined alternatives.

Why, then, is fingering so commonly neglected? The best answer is probably that the student is not compelled to use any one fingering in order to play the right notes, at least to play them "after a fashion." He soon discovers that he can get by without reading the editor's fingering—if, indeed, he even notices that it is there. To be sure, by dint of repeated playings he does quickly fall into some sort of fingering that becomes habitual with him. But there lies the rub. The fingering he falls into is almost certain not to be the best fingering. Experimentation is required to discover the technical superiority of one fingering over another, and over-all planning is required to make the fingering consistent.

The ideal solution to careless fingering and the most constructive approach, in any case, is to have the student work out his own fingering from the first piece he plays. He should get started on this just as soon as he has given his new piece enough readings to get the general idea but not enough readings to establish bad habits. (And a word of caution is needed here, for bad habits of fingering have a way of establishing themselves with remarkably few playings, only to reappear in a most agonizing manner and on the most unexpected occasions.) I should like to urge that as much as the first quarter of the time spent on learning a new piece be devoted to an exhaustive consideration and final selection of the best possible fingering. The close study that this entails, with the hands considered separately and the music examined by sections, is, in fact, the best possible insurance that the new piece will have a rock-bottom foundation. Furthermore, it is my belief that the early lessons on a new piece ought to center around the fingering brought in by the student, at

which time the student may perhaps be shown still further and
more practical solutions.

As to how the student goes about his fingering, some remarks
may be offered that should prove useful. First of all, it would be
best if he could play from editions that have not already been
fingered by the editor. Then he could reach his own decisions
without prejudice. However, most editions are published with
fingering, the notable exceptions being *Urtext* editions and many
recent publications, especially those from France. His attitude,
when he encounters editorial fingerings, should be one of interest
and hard skepticism. The editor's fingering may represent
enormous, valuable experience, as it does, for example, in
Joseffy's edition of Chopin. But more often than not it represents
the hasty work of a dollar-a-page man—the kind who edits
repeated passages differently and omits the fingerings that call
for experienced judgment; or it represents the fingerings of a
man with a hand of a different size and with different notions
as to how such fundamentals as the trill, the chromatic scale,
and repeated notes are to be played. The student should systematically try out every possible fingering that he can find, making
certain that among these has been the editor's solution. Often he
can discover the best solutions by working back from the end
of a passage, just as a writer of mystery stories may work back
from the end of a plot. If, after considering the various determining factors, he finds no one best fingering, then an arbitrary
decision must be made. The problem is not necessarily to find
the one best fingering so much as to find a good, usable fingering
to which he can faithfully adhere.

When the student has decided upon a fingering, he should,
without fail, write it in, placing it unambiguously near the note
it concerns in clear, small figures. He will do best to use a light
pencil with a good eraser. The fingering must be written in,
both for the obvious reason that it would otherwise be forgotten

in practice and for the less obvious one that written fingering is a great expediter when the piece is relearned at a later time. This last is more than an advantage; it is virtually a necessity for relearning. The habit of a particular fingering sticks much better than the recollection of it. When a pianist tries to relearn a piece that he had failed to finger in writing, he usually finds himself struggling with fingering that fights against the old habits he cannot recall.

Just how much fingering to put in requires good judgment, too. If every note is figured the fingering becomes a major obstacle in reading. The rule should be to put in fingering wherever and only wherever there can be any chance of ambiguity, then or later. The student tends to put too much fingering in passage work and too little in chords and chordal accompaniments. If the right-hand thumb lights on c′ and the passage progresses diatonically up to g′, there is normally no need to put in anything but 1 for the thumb. He may assume, that is, that the fingers will succeed each other in their natural order and a note at a time unless fingering is put in to the contrary. Thus, if the same c′ were fingered with the second finger at least one other figure would be needed to show the way up to g′. Chords give the impression that no choice of fingering is possible. Actually, there is very often an alternative between 3 and 4 or 4 and 5 that directly concerns the ease of playing. A common instance is the waltz (um-pah-pah) accompaniment, in which the fifth finger of the left hand is often best saved for the bass while the other fingers play the afterbeats with the fingering that comes nearest to stretching both bass and afterbeats as one chord. This fifth-finger bass, incidentally, can be aimed more accurately by approaching it as though the thumb were to play the octave above, too, and eying not the fifth finger but the thumb.

From what has been said, the importance of sticking to a

fingering after it has been worked out must be very apparent. Occasionally further familiarity with the fingering will bring out unanticipated difficulties, necessitating changes that are hard to get used to. However, the student may prepare somewhat for such contingencies by testing his fingering both for more strength and more speed than he is likely to need in performance. In planning his fingering, he must realize that the ultimate speed may mean not only a greater but a different technical problem.

A major factor in the practicability of a fingering is its simplicity. Over and over again, a complex fingering that plays neatly and cleanly when the section is isolated becomes a mental hazard to concentration and memorizing when the piece is played through. An example is the clever fingering of turns and other ornaments that one often encounters; usually the simple 3-2-1-2 for the four-note turn and the 3-2 or 3-1 for the trill prove to be the safest and surest solutions. Another example is the excessive exchange of two fingers on a single note in order to achieve a legato that might come much easier by adroit pedaling. Another is the habit of changing fingers on repeated notes in slow to moderate tempos, when one finger propelled by wrist action would prove to be much simpler. Still another example occurs in the sequential repetition of a short melodic pattern. The fingering that works well at one point in the sequence does not work so well at another. Nevertheless, the mental security gained by not having to watch for the finger change usually outweighs the slight advantage of the better fingering. Scale and arpeggio passages should ordinarily follow the standard scale and arpeggio fingerings to avoid confusion. One is inviting trouble, for example, to play a scale in A major with 1-2-3-4 1-2-3 rather than the usual 1-2-3 1-2-3-4 unless something else about the passage makes this change necessary.

As an interesting example of how helpful a clear and simple mental concept of the fingering can be, try repeating the succession D, C#, E♭, C# rapidly in the right hand, using the first fingering that comes to mind. Note what a "tongue twister" this is. Now play this succession with the fingering 1-2-3-2. Think of it as a three-finger exercise, concentrating on the natural order of the fingers rather than the irregular order of the keys, and note how simple it becomes.

A second factor in practical fingering is use of the strongest fingers for the strongest accents in the meter or other groupings. Thus, among numerous fingerings illustrated in our fifth chapter are uses of both the thumb and fifth finger on black keys at either end of an arpeggio figure. In spite of the strange look and feel of this fingering, it provides excellent strength and security on the extreme notes and few or none of the humps that might be expected with so brazen a defiance of the old rule about avoiding the thumb on a black key. That rule, by the way, still casts its shadow on pianists' fingering, wrongly discouraging them from many very sensible uses of the thumb for strength and accuracy. Thus, the thumb can save the day by rapid slides from black to white keys or by covering adjacent keys in wide chords (as in Ex. 21). And, pointed down with fingers clenched, it can transmit arm attacks to a single bass tone that are too much for the fifth finger (if not the string!). Both the choice and the strength of fingering are also affected by decisions as to which hand should be marked "over" or "under" when one of them crosses the other or straddles it (as often in Debussy and Ravel).

A third factor in good fingering is consistency. Similar passages ought normally to be fingered similarly if the performer does not want to do twice as much work. Besides, if he does finger them differently he will find that the similar passages confuse each other in performance, meaning that the performer must be constantly on guard to remember which time he intended which fingering. Naturally, some latitude must be allowed because the similar passages are often not so similar that identical fingering can be used. But then the very difference in the passage helps the pianist to remember the difference in the fingering, and conversely. In fact, there is even an occasion when he might deliberately use an altogether different fingering. That happens when one passage leads back to the beginning again and the same or a similar passage leads on to a new section, as often happens in a rondo. Then the alertness required to change the fingering is a wise precaution. (I recall how the excellent Viennese pianist Severin Eisenberger, while playing one of several recitals that covered all thirty-two of Beethoven's sonatas, started to go round and round at just such a passage in the rondo of the easy G major sonata, Op. 49, finally giving up and walking off in exasperation!)

One other factor in practical fingering is the number of successive notes that can be covered ahead of time. Other things being equal, it is wise to have the fingering cover as many of the coming notes as possible in one grasp of the hand. This reduces the number of thumb shifts and promotes that streamlined, well-planted, solid style of playing sometimes known as "position technique" (related to the practice of "clusters," previously discussed under Technique). Such fingering will often contradict the interruptions that editors deliberately make in fingering (for example, ascending on the white keys by 3-4-5 2-3-4) so as to compel the separation of slurs and phrases.

COUNTING AND RHYTHM, THE KEY TO AUTHORITATIVE PLAYING

Others have said it, and here it is again: "In the beginning there was rhythm." One might add, "Everybody complains but nobody does anything about it." One of the most important musical subjects is also one of the most elusive; hence the dearth of careful studies on rhythm, the frequent glossing over when it must be mentioned in other studies. (Here I hasten to interject:

Neither is this the long-awaited study.) Rhythm, being along with pitch one of the two essentials of music, seems to underlie all musical problems. Just as many apparent physical ailments prove to stem from psychosomatic problems, so many apparent faults in technique, interpretation, and memory prove to stem from rhythmic problems.

It is surprising, for example, to discover how much the metronome alone will cure when used to regulate the counting. The teacher wears himself out trying to correct this quirk and that hesitation in his student, yet the minute one fault rights itself

another appears, as if the problem were to repair the oft-cited leaky bag. At last he thinks of the metronome, the student works with it, begins to get the swing of the music, and everything clears up like magic. I have known even violinists to correct their intonation when the rhythmic (and therefore the harmonic) structure is clarified for them by the use of the metronome.

The metronome is often condemned, incidentally, by those who fear the mechanical results it will produce. There is that danger, without a doubt. But let this much be said. The student who cannot and does not practice with the metronome up to the point where he can stay with it—and that is all he needs to do—is in the far greater danger of not understanding what he plays at all. As a sort of robot teacher during parts of the practice session, the metronome is a "must" for every serious student in spite of its relatively high purchase price.

The single most important thing the student can do about his rhythm, from the practical standpoint of this book, is to count. He should count the meter aloud in clear, crisp tones—not chant in weird, sustained tones, because then he is not defining the beats. He should not subdivide the beat with "ands" unless the tempo is actually so slow as to need subdivision—that is, where the use of "ands" is essential to the flow of the protracted beats. Otherwise, "ands" break up the beat, lose the sense of flow, and so defeat one important purpose of counting. Only when there is an irregular subdivision of the beat, as with dotted rhythms or the long and short notes of a triplet, may it be necessary to fill in the subdivisions temporarily. Thus, the student might count *one-de-de-de* to locate ♩♪ or ♫♪ correctly, but only on the beats where these occur. Such subdivisions often suffer distressing neglect. How ruinous to the heart of the rhythmic structure is the conversion of triplets into ♫♪ or dotted patterns into ♪♪ !

Tapping the foot of course does not answer as a substitute for counting aloud, both because the foot must be free to pedal, and to pedal independently of the rhythm, and because the voice can keep track of the position in the measure by numbering the beats. The one rule governing the question when to count is simply this: The student must count everything he plays until he can say every count without confusion. Then the counting has done its work. But he must be on the watch for absent-minded mumbling in the place of counting, or the occasional omission of a count, for these are not accidents but positive evidences of rhythmic confusion and lack of control.

The reason for counting must be understood. The student must realize that effective rhythm depends on the opposition of two factors, 1) the underlying pulse or beat and 2) the pattern of notes that is superimposed on that pulse. If he taps his foot while he whistles "Stars and Stripes Forever," for instance, he will note how the foot gives the pulse while the whistling sounds the pattern. To turn this fact into practice, that is, to play with *rhythmic authority*, he must be able to feel both pulse and pattern simultaneously. This is what is accomplished by counting aloud while playing.

The student understands why he must get the pattern right (although he often has to be shown what "feeling it" means). So much he sees on the printed page and plays with his fingers. But he is likely to fall down on the counting unless this is supervised. The counting represents a pulse of definitely physical origin—a steady throb that takes place in the involuntary visceral muscles, so we are told. The act of counting aloud must be regarded as an exaggeration of what the student will later say to himself and of the pulse that he will come to feel inside. Mr. Loesser, who never fails to infuse his playing with rhythmic vitality, adds here,

> "I have found it useful to tell students to think of music not as a bunch of notes arranged into a rhythmic pattern, but rather as a skeleton of beats on which the notes are set, like the jewels on a sunburst. A note may be defined as something that fits on a beat, a sound that must be placed on its own exclusive *time-spot*. First come beats, then notes.
>
> "Another useful suggestion is that instrumental music is, basically, dance music. For the most part it must sound 'dancy,' slow movements as well as fast; if it doesn't, it will sound unhappy.

Playing in time is not a penance, or even a discipline; it is just fun, just dancing."

Setting the pulse properly means getting into the *swing* of the music. We see this in the extreme when the jazz band leader sets the beat before his men start in by jogging at the shoulders and knees. A sense of swing can usually be trained, or rather, brought out, though students differ extraordinarily in their sense of pulse. (A student weak in rhythm often shows this weakness on the dance floor or in the marching band.) The overly shy, inhibited student is at a disadvantage because he is often reluctant to express himself in the energetic, muscular manner that the swing of the music requires. He must be made to understand that whatever may be the merits of shyness in other living, piano playing is one activity where that shyness must be circumvented.

Undoubtedly, the physical interpretation of rhythmic patterns and pulses through Dalcroze Eurythmics, or similar dance movements, helps to alleviate rhythmic apathy. Just how much it actually carries over to the problems of piano playing is hard to say. In any case, the student who succeeds in feeling and controlling the pulse in conjunction with the rhythmic pattern, who succeeds in bringing his rhythms to life, may congratulate himself on graduating from the large mass of pianists who play dully and indifferently because they play without this rhythmic authority.

Although many teachers will agree that a fair share of their energies goes into getting across the rhythm ♩ ♪ and similar basic patterns, the fact remains that most children of five and six can learn to count the principal note values. A simple method of accustoming the student to the interrelation of the metric pulses and the note values in a new piece is to have him count the pulse aloud and clap the notes wherever they occur. This is fun for him and comes close enough to the actual experience of playing the piece to result in direct good. If the student continues to distort the rhythm, a further help is to have him memorize the rhythm of a specific passage, then walk to it as he claps it and counts the pulse. The regularity of the walking is certain to show up any discrepancies in the pulse and therefore in the rhythmic pattern. The metronome will accomplish the same purpose, of course, though the physical nature of the pulse will not then be so apparent to the student.

The most complex rhythms to figure out mathematically—and figured out they must be, without fail—are those with many black notes, flags, beams, double dots, and ties, such as are found in slow movements rather than allegro movements. Familiar examples are the introductions to Beethoven's Sonata *Pathétique* and Liszt's *Hungarian Rhapsody* No. 12. Students also have difficulty in distinguishing the two or more sets of rhythms that belong to up- and down-stem melodies written on the same staff. They must figure these out, of course, in order to know how long each finger holds its note. The most complex rhythms to do in performance are those with constant metric changes and energetic syncopations, as in the faster, dancelike movements of Aaron Copland.

Time signatures are fractions best translated into "this many (numerator) of these (denominator) in a measure," the numerator telling the number of pulses and the denominator the value of each. Thus, to translate $\frac{3}{4}$ the student only needs to say, "There are *three quarters* (fourths) in a measure." This method suffices for "simple" meters but must be amplified for "compound" meters, in which the denominator is compounded by threes in all but the slower tempos. The distinction between simple meter, with its pulse that subdivides by twos, and compound meter, with its invariably dotted pulse that subdivides by threes, is something all too many musicians fail to get clear. To translate such signatures all the way, merely divide the numerator by three and multiply the denominator by three (remembering the denominator is a fourth or an eighth, etc., not four or eight). Thus, $\frac{9}{8}$ or $\frac{6}{4}$ at moderate to fast tempos really means $\hat{r}$ or $\hat{r}$. Our present system of metric notation has no other means (aside from triplet signs) of indicating regular ternary pulses. "Cut" or *alla breve* meter, $\frac{2}{2}$ or ¢, is unusual in having a compound pulse that subdivides by two. Irregular meters imply irregular compounds ($\frac{5}{8} = \downarrow + \downarrow.$).

The physical nature of rhythmic feeling is important in another respect beside pulse, or rather in another aspect of pulse, which is tempo. Tempo means rate of speed. It is one more of those very elusive elements in rhythm. So elusive, in fact, that many have despaired of writing about it. In our fifth chapter some clues are offered for finding the most appropriate tempo in any one piece. The problem is to determine just how fast Mozart intended a certain andante movement to be played, or Scarlatti a certain presto movement, or merely the approximate speed in the many Bach compositions that contain no tempo designations at all. So it is that the one thing for which a conductor may be safely criticized with reasonable impunity is his tempo in this or that composition.

Of course, much of the music written later, in the nineteenth and twentieth centuries, is supplied with metronome speeds by the composer, and most earlier music is so marked by modern editors. These indications are indeed very specific but they have three main faults. First, they are often open to question both because composers are notoriously bad guessers as to exactly what tempos best suit their music, and because the editor represents, after all, just another man's judgment. Second, they give a mechanical idea of speed but fail entirely to impart the physical feeling for the particular tempo. And third, they are too specific because tempo undoubtedly varies with the prevailing mood and the occasion. (For instance, the time required for sound to travel through the air may necessitate a slower tempo in a very large room than would be used in a small room.)

To a seasoned orchestra conductor I am indebted for what seems to me to be the most musical way to arrive at the five basic tempos of music, which are: adagio, largo, andante, allegro, and presto. These five terms originated in Italian as designations for styles of physical movement from very slow to very fast. They may be translated as very slow, slow, moderate, fast, very fast, though this gives no hint of their psychological character. As used by the great composers, they are ordinarily more dependable and meaningful than metronome markings. Each tempo may be *felt* by associating it with a familiar walking step, as is indicated in the following table. (Unfortunately, the meanings of adagio and largo are sometimes interchanged, and the other terms have often been used with different intentions; but the sense of this discussion still applies.)

Table of Tempos

Adagio. The delayed step done in a funeral march, down the aisle at a wedding, or at a graduation procession. So slow that it must be divided, in order to avoid faltering, by holding each foot back until it rises to its ball-of-the-foot at the middle of the count. Count with "ands" in order to subdivide the beat. Example: the *Funeral March* (marked *Lento*, which is often equivalent to adagio) from Chopin's Sonata in B-flat minor.

Largo. The regal, sedate step used at a stately ceremonial or in the walk of a condemned man. As slow as can be taken without faltering or subdividing. Count one for each beat, without subdivision. Example: Dvořák's *Largo* from the *New World* Symphony.

Andante. The relaxed step used in a leisurely Sunday afternoon stroll or a Fifth Avenue window-shopping tour. Moderate and flowing, done without lifting the heel. Count one to each beat. Example: the *Andante Cantabile* from Tschaikowsky's Fifth Symphony.

Allegro. The brisk step of a businessman walking to work on time but not ahead of time; in between the marching cadence of Army troops and of most football bands. It is characterized by its spring and energy, sometimes including a take-off from the ball of the foot. Count one to each beat (or each metric unit in "cut" time). Example: Brahms's *Rhapsody* in G minor.

Presto. When counted one to a beat, a short, mincing step taken almost at a run, as by a puppet or mechanical doll. So fast that it can be done only on the toes and with straight legs. Count one to an entire measure in simple time, one to a dotted unit or entire measure in compound time, up to the number of measures in a phrase or rhythmic group. Example: Mendelssohn's *Spinning Song.*

An interesting and revealing evidence of rhythmic insecurity is the bobbing of the head that many students will do when they are hard pressed to stay with the metronome or preoccupied with some difficulty in the notes. This is a bad habit that must be eliminated both by direct criticism and by tracing the rhythmic deficiency. It usually indicates that the player is trying to make up for a hitch in his realization of the pulse. In what was at the time a most humiliating experience, the wrongness of this habit was firmly impressed on me. I was still in my teens when I was invited to play a Handel harpsichord concerto with the Cleveland Symphony Orchestra (the "harpsichord" provided at that time was merely a "prepared" Steinway with metal-tipped hammers). At the first rehearsal I showed up with all the cockiness of inexperience. As soon as the first downbeat landed, I commenced all manner of energetic bobbings so as to keep pace with the conductor and the orchestra. It was only a matter of minutes before Nikolai Sokoloff, then the conductor, tapped his desk, stopped the orchestra, and slowly turned around to bellow, "What are you trying to do? Lead the orchestra?" Thoroughly chagrined, I telephoned the assistant conductor that night to learn what I had done wrong. The reply was simple. Orchestra players quickly learn that head and body movements *on the beat* only tend to throw the players off the beat and produce a muddy ensemble.

Generally speaking, such movements in excess of technical requirements are like all mannerisms in performance, including facial grimaces, breathy grunts, and flopping arms. They attempt to make up for something not quite achieved in the music itself. Furthermore, they are distracting to the audience, which usually admires the quiet, businesslike performer who lets the music speak altogether for itself. It is worth noting that at the most intense and dramatic moments performers sit fairly still, anyway, because they are too busy to move and because they dare not shift the base for their aim, so to speak.

There are, however, a few occasions when rhythmic movements by the head or body seem more justified. An experienced player may make a slight buoyant or lilting movement from the trunk as he figuratively dances along with the beat. Or he may jerk his head on a missing beat, as in a syncopation, which tempts even the listener to reach out and supply that beat. If a rhythmic player must beware an occasional audible grunt at such places, an arrhythmic one must be urged to do his "loudest playing" on tied notes, dots, and rests, and he must recall that such rhythmic life presupposes alert, not slumped, posture.

Furthermore, in very slow music where there is a problem of keeping the flow going throughout the phrase and especially during rests, the player might try making exactly one steady clockwise rotation from the trunk for each phrase. This movement serves much like the curlicues and dips of the baton that a conductor makes at slow tempos in order to keep the beat flowing and to avoid delayed, abrupt strokes that would take his men by surprise. Students should be encouraged to make such rotary movements when they show an inclination to fidget or to be bored with their own playing in very slow tempos. Otherwise they tend to speed up and to miss the meaning of the long, even line of the phrase. Unfortunately, just as the art of writing noble, sustained slow music seems to be on the wane (though there are some heartening recent exceptions), so the art of playing it seems to be disappearing. No doubt, the pace and intensity of our everyday living has something to do with this fact, for the audiences are similarly losing their patience with slow movements. If this should actually prove to be the trend, there could hardly be a worse loss to music!

INTERPRETATION: THE SUM OF UNDERSTANDING, EXPERIENCE, AND TALENT

Music is one of the time arts. This means that, unlike the space arts—painting, sculpture, and architecture—music must be brought back to life by a new projection in time on every occasion that it is to be appreciated. There must be a middleman between producer and consumer who returns to the mute notation on the printed page in order to re-create the creations of the composer. This act is what is meant by interpretation. Its purpose, in short, is to convey the meaning and intentions of the composer, both intellectual and expressive.

Effective, convincing interpretation presupposes three attributes on the part of the interpreter: experience, understanding, and musicality or native talent. It will be understood, then, why interpretation seems like such an indefinable subject, why the teacher tends to stop at that point, saying to the student, "From here on, either you can or you cannot." Interpretation is really the intangible sum of everything else that goes to make up piano playing, of everything that is discussed here, for that matter. And it includes other things, too. It includes all that goes to make up personality, quite apart from problems of piano practice and performance, for out of our personality we get the predispositions that determine our tastes. In spite of a well-known statement to the contrary, notation is still only implicit rather than explicit, and a great deal in the matter of taste is left to the performer, even in the music most scrupulously edited by the composer. It is no wonder, then, that interpretations can differ so widely without losing their validity at either extreme. This latitude, which makes possible the continual refreshment of music, is, in fact, the principal reason why art remains beautiful, mysterious, and unchained.

Of the three prerequisites to effective interpretation mentioned, only understanding can be considered here. Actual experience and innate musicality do not come from a book. Over and above the knowledge required to read, count, finger, and manage the notes, there is one further aspect of understanding that matters particularly in interpretation. That is the understanding of form. Form includes whatever binds the music into a unified structure, whether it be tonality, rhythm, melody, or, as is usually the case, a combination of all three. The student's problem is to determine which of these predominates and how; or, to put it colloquially, What makes the piece tick?

He will not need a course in form and analysis, desirable as that would be, to discover the reiterations of a fugue subject, the return of a rondo theme, the digression in an ABA design, or the simple variation of a melody. Nor will he have undue difficulties in detecting varieties of rhythmic treatment. He *will* need at least a rudimentary foundation in harmony, which he needs anyway for his daily playing, to recognize the tonal scheme of a Haydn sonata or the three or four cadences in nearly related keys that outline a Bach invention. With what background and ability he has to perceive form traits, the student will greatly benefit himself by jotting down in the score whatever he can find on his own. This analysis he should submit to the teacher for discussion, along with the fingering that has been worked out, at one of the first lessons on a new piece. True, the gist of his findings might eventually impress itself on his senses without the conscious analysis. But, how much easier for him, as for the animal seeking food in the psychologist's maze, if the right doors are opened in advance.

An understanding of form is an important means of arriving at a *concept of the whole* in performance, which is, strangely, one of the most neglected and yet one of the most vital aspects of interpretation. Even established performers will play through extended compositions with remarkable attention to detail and little or no sense of the broad interrelation of large sections. They will fail, for example, to perceive the climaxes on a comparative basis, or will lose track of the prevailing tempo, or do each return to a theme in the same manner, or make a sudden dynamic thrust, such as an extra loud final chord, that is wholly out of keeping with the general level of the piece.

Here, as in other piano problems, the metronome may be of some help, for its use can highlight the over-all form of a piece that has a single or prevailing tempo by integrating its diverse rhythms. Yet this is only the beginning. In music before Haydn and Mozart—that is, before the time when composers generally put interpretative markings in their music, the student has an exceptional opportunity to advance an original concept of the whole piece. He can use an *Urtext* edition or disregard editorial markings to work out and enter his own plan for the dynamics. ("Laying the groundwork" is illustrated in this and other respects in the fifth chapter.) The large sections of the form might be set off well by only one contrasting sign per section—perhaps an *f*, *mf*, or *p*, producing what the Germans call "terrace dynamics."

So much concerns the primarily intellectual aspect of the dynamics. Next, the student can attend to the expressive details. Here he must realize that a continual, undulating series of short crescendos and diminuendos is by no means a guarantee of intelligent, musical interpretation. Such well-meant but often sentimental swells, usually done in slavishly regular phrases, can easily disrupt the broader flow. Add undue rubato, especially any hastening of pulses, and pure *Schmalz* occurs (the musician's very piquant term). Interpretation has larger goals. Expressive details are most valid when they bear out the emotional import of the whole composition and when they point up the form by drawing attention to its focal points, as to a cadence, a new idea, a climax, or a breathing spot.

Where detailed interpretation within broad sections is concerned, the chief problem is the shaping of the phrase. Phrases, like sentences, are so variable in their make-up that one would suppose no generalizations about their performance would hold. Yet, from French theorists, who have contributed importantly to the understanding of expression and rhythm, come certain guides to intelligent phrasing, guides of great value to the performer. They are especially helpful to the student whose imagination is not yet trained to see the possibilities, and in music of the more established styles and forms.

By its very definition, the phrase has a beginning, a climactic point (point of maximum intensity), and an ending. Just as the sentence may have one or more subordinate clauses, so the phrase may have one or more lesser climaxes. The first problem of the student, however, is to determine the main climactic point, toward and away from which the whole phrase should move. The rise and fall of the melody is often given as a clue to the increase and decrease of intensity in a phrase. This is a natural tendency of the voice and of many wind and string instruments that are most penetrating and brilliant in their high ranges. Many times it actually proves to be the true significance of the phrase in piano music, but, of course, just as many times it does

Ex. 22

Permission for reprint granted by copyright owners, Durand et Cie, Paris, and Elkan-Vogel Company, Inc., Philadelphia.

not. Brahms, for instance, will often increase the volume as he spins out a rich melody that descends into its lowest tones. For a more comprehensive guide the following two principles are recommended:

1) In a phrase that contains some unusual feature, that feature becomes the climactic point. The feature may be an unusually

expressive harmony, remote foreign tone, long tone, high tone, low tone, or an unexpected dynamic marking, provided that it occurs in a way that permits adequate emphasis (for example, that it is not of too short duration). The climactic point in such a phrase may even occur on the first or last note (disregarding, here, the contention that all phrases begin on an actual or implied upbeat), as often in Debussy. Ex. 22 shows three instances of unusual climactic points (marked c.p.) in the phrase.

2) Otherwise the climactic point of the phrase normally occurs on the last strong beat *before* the final note. The strong beat, in this sense, is usually the first beat of the measure, though in slow music it may be the middle of a $\frac{4}{4}$ measure or any of the dotted-unit beats in a compound measure. Ex. 23 shows two instances of "normally" located climactic points:

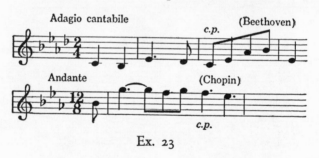

Ex. 23

More often than not the two principles co-operate, confirming the choice of climactic point or, rather, leaving none, especially when the last strong beat coincides with a focal dissonance (as in the Chopin phrase). Otherwise, questions as to which is the last strong beat, and the like, still leave considerable latitude for interpretation even among the authorities (as in the Beethoven phrase, with A-flat or the first E-flat as alternative climactic points). At least, the student now has some basis for his decisions. Yet before these must come answers to this question: What *is* a phrase? How do you mark off musical ideas that vary as widely in length and structure as sentences?

In a good deal of stereotyped music, and in much other music as well, there is the same kind of symmetrical inevitability that one expects to find in a Limerick. In such music the student merely needs to check his phrases off at regular, usually at four-measure, intervals. But in a large part of the serious music he will play, irregular phrase syntax is the rule rather than the exception. There are elisions, extensions, overlappings, chain sequences, and truncations without end. Composers like Haydn and Hindemith revel in them. What is the student to do? A detailed answer cannot be given here. But a choice may remain, anyway, for after all the irregularities have been classified, one must still return to the definition that a phrase is a musical idea. It is a complete idea, yet it is but a fragment in the larger organization just as it itself is made up of smaller fragments.

The French theorists say that the primordial atoms in this whole scheme are two- and three-note figures (incises) that overlap a bar line (or ictus) by moving from weak to strong beat, or from weak through strong to weak beat. These may be represented in $\frac{3}{4}$ meter, for instance, as 123⌢123 or 123|1⌢23; and in $\frac{4}{4}$ meter as 1234⌢1234 or 1234|12⌢34, and so forth. For concrete examples, recall the seven two-note groups and the three three-note groups that respectively make up the phrases "Mine eyes have seen the glory of the coming of the Lord" and "My bonnie lies over the ocean." Even in these short figures there must be rise and fall, for they are but miniatures of the complete phrase. It is obvious that in the two-note figure (usually termed masculine) the rise must occur on the first note (arsis) and the fall on the second (thesis); and in the three-note figure (feminine) the rise must occur on the first note, reaching a peak on the second note, followed by a fall on the third note.

In the sense that energy is required to rise rather than to fall, the first note in each figure, although it occurs on the so-called weak beat, is really a point of lift or expressive stress. This fact, which may sound to the student like just so much detail, is actually of the greatest importance to intelligent phrasing, and one that is very commonly neglected. It applies, for example, to the innumerable two- and three-note slurs, which are among the identification tags of the Mozart style. Furthermore, this principle is the basis for the lift that should announce each new phrase and, in a larger sense, for the lift that characterizes the "A" sections of the various two-part (AB) and three-part (ABA) forms.

An allied and interrelated process can be seen in tonal movement. The two-note group is supported by a chord of suspense on the "weak" beat and a chord of repose on the "strong" beat. In the larger sense of the AB form, the rise becomes the modulation to the dominant, and the fall the return to the tonic. In the three-note group, the harmony creates suspense, dissonance, and resolution, while in the sections of the ABA form the tonality rises to the dominant, tours through other keys, and returns.

A phrase usually consists of several two- or three-note groups. In shape it normally resembles the three- rather than the two-note group. This should be realized because we tend to think of the phrase as an arch with the climactic point in the center. Actually, it is more likely to resemble a streamlined auto fender, with the high point coming at the observer's right (near the end). For the performer this means that the rounding off, or what might be called the low point of the phrase, must take place much quicker than the long rise to the climactic point. This gives him concern because at best it is harder to play soft than loud. Yet the rounding off is a prime requisite of good phrasing and just as important as the sense of lift at the beginning. It is like sinking into a deep sofa after a hike. To omit it is as frustrating and shocking as to have the sofa break through.

Indeed, abrupt thrusts at the ends of phrases are among the most glaring evidences of musical insensitivity. Especially in a slow phrase with a feminine ending, the performer should try to play the final note no louder than the volume to which the previous note has died away.

In determining the shape and extent of each phrase the student must not be misled by editorial slurs that pertain not to phrases but to legato passages. While the two uses are sometimes synonymous, their confusion represents one of the serious faults in our notation system. The confusion is even worse for other mediums, where slurs indicate breathing, bowing, and syllabification! Various suggestions have been offered for marking off the phrases, especially the nonlegato sort that dare not have a slur over them for fear they will be played legato. None of these suggestions has attained general use. Therefore, the student must consider the slurs with caution and be prepared to do his own phrase marking, with the good counsel of his teacher.

Besides an understanding of form and phrasing, interpretation calls for a familiarity with the styles of different composers, different eras, and different moods. This familiarity is a direct outcome of long experience. It also depends on a knowledge of authenticity in style. There, from the pianist's standpoint, is where the musicologist can be of greatest service. The musicologist restores the music to its original form so that we can distinguish the composer's intentions from all the editorial trappings and alterations that have accumulated over the years. Then he reports on the performance practices of different eras so that we can be faithful, within reason, to the composer's implications. I say "within reason" because the farther back we go the harder it is to reproduce the music exactly as it was meant. After all, most of us play the piano, not the harpsichord or clavichord. On the piano we can simulate the idea of the music only as the piano permits. The piano is simply a different instrument with its own advantages and deficiencies. Too faithful a reproduction of the older music, such as one occasionally meets in harpsichord "transcriptions" for piano, with their awkward imitations of couplings, can only be ridiculous.

Ornaments are among the most vexing and most violated of performance practices. Up to the time of Clementi and Chopin, when composers began to write them out, they were indicated by a large variety of unstandardized signs, whose interpretation depended on the period, the locale, the composer, and above all, the context of the music. The serious student who delves deep into the music of the Bach period must expect not only to consult the best editors but to engage in a certain amount of research on his own. Then he will be better qualified to do what must be done in the last analysis anyway, and that is to use his own best judgment.

Properly executed, ornaments add great charm and spice to the music. Some of them cannot be done properly at all on the piano because of the heavier action. A few basic principles that are still widely disregarded may be repeated here, for the period from Bach to Mozart. Their applications to actual situations are varied, however. Some specific examples by Bach and others are taken up in the fifth chapter. For further details the reader may consult sources such as the *Harvard Dictionary of Music* (recommended earlier for a basic music library), where he will find illustrated articles on each ornament, or performing editions in which practical solutions are recommended (such as my own editions listed on the title-page of this book).

1) Trills in the music from Bach to Mozart generally begin on the upper note and on the beat. Sometimes an approach from the note below the principal note is indicated, but rarely does the trill begin on the principal note itself. Trills may or may not continue throughout the note over which they are written and may or may not terminate with a windup. Sometimes these

variants are indicated; more often they are left to the performer's good discretion. When the trill occurs on the beat, as with other ornaments, part of the purpose is to create spice through dissonance. This fact may help to determine the starting note. A large number of signs are used to indicate the trill, often with no distinction intended. In Bach, the zigzag sign commonly mistaken for an inverted mordent means a trill. The inverted mordent is so rare in music of that period (chiefly in the course of descending scale passages) that every use of it must be seriously questioned before it is accepted. The turn should be thought of as a trill that commences from above or below the principal tone (as the sign makes clear) and concludes with a windup from below.

2) Appoggiaturas (leaning notes) in the same music begin on the beat and receive part of the value of the principal note that is written on the beat. Just what part of the value is the chief problem. It can be all the way from almost nothing (like the modern grace note if played on the beat) to the entire value (when the principal note is followed by a rest). Two guides are helpful in many instances, though the composers cannot be counted on to observe them. One is to give the appoggiatura its written value. The other is to give it half the value of the principal note unless the latter is dotted, then two thirds of the value.

Good taste in the matter of dynamics also depends on a knowledge of styles. The "terrace" dynamics mentioned hold good primarily for the Bach period and still exert force in the Mozart and Haydn period. (Such dynamics make good training for the student who monotonously plays everything on the same level. In Scarlatti, for example, he may be asked to start by playing everything *either loud or soft*, but not in between.) Yet it would be wrong to think of delicate nuance and tasteful rubato as the exclusive province of the nineteenth-century Romanticists. The good taste consists of staying within bounds and knowing the bounds. The volume that seems necessary to Liszt will seem hard and overdone for Mozart.

What is more, the very method of achieving volume varies. In allegro passages by Mozart, as in most lively, strongly rhythmic music, volume is more a matter of the number of metric accents than of the degree of stress. Thus, two groups of four sixteenths each might be played *piano* by using no accents: *pppp pppp*, played *mezzo forte* by using one accent: *fppp pppp*, played *forte* by accenting the first of each group: *fppp fppp*, and *fortissimo*, by accenting every other note: *fpfp fpfp*. On the other hand, in stentorian passages by Liszt, as in other very dramatic music, each note is played very fully. To a large extent these differences are rhythmic in origin. Fast music moves along in groups of notes; slow music requires that each note get individual emphasis, the grouping being present but less conspicuous.

Style and taste both touch on virtually everything else in piano playing too; much more than could possibly be discussed here. The playing of contrapuntal music, for example, raises fascinating problems of proper emphasis, of clear distinction between lines, of overlapping rhythms. To "right-handed" pianists, steeped in homophonic waltzes and nocturnes, this type of playing opens wholly new horizons. In both contrapuntal and homophonic music, the force and sense of the harmony is enhanced by intelligent emphasis on the most influential tones at the moment of each chord change. These tones are more readily identified when they are foreign to the key and hence preceded by accidentals (as in the Mozart phrase of Ex. 22).

The distinction in degrees of staccato and legato needs constant attention. In slow music, the crisp staccato of a quick piece is ordinarily out of place. In quick music, even the ends of slurs are assumed to be staccato. In a Scarlatti run, the velvety legato of a Chopin *fioritura* (florid, ornamental passage) is usually inappropriate. The endless variety of nuance required in poetic performance demands a wealth of attacks, expressive delays, *subito pianos* (called "Beethoven piano" when it "tops" a crescendo and often done into the ground as a mannerism), and bold accents. These might almost be termed the performer's bag of tricks from which he draws, as a Heifetz or a Kreisler selects from his endless variety of violin tones.

The balance of effects in a composition calls for a fine sense of timing, as well as the perspective of musical structure already discussed. In slow movements there is ordinarily time for much grander, more sustained climaxes than in quick movements, where the climaxes are likely to be more passionate and spectacular. In cumulative sections there must be breathing spaces where the performer can draw back for his Sunday punch—as Beethoven, Brahms, and Wagner knew so well. He must learn to take one step back for each two forward in order to prolong the climax. Romantic music typically builds around the concept of *the one climax*, often achieved by *the one* consummating harmony. This climax typically appears near the end—recall Wagner's *Tristan* or the Rachmaninoff Piano Concertos or the Strauss songs—, often followed by a brief, quiet coda, thus reproducing the "auto fender" type curve in a vastly larger sense.

Whether a climax or drop comes soon or later, students tend to reach it *too* soon. Recall the familiar caution that *cresc.* and *decresc.* or $\prec$ and $\succ$ mean louder or softer *later on*. Often, too, every climax is made a maximum effort, especially in the flurry of a concert. Giving one's all is a bit like losing one's temper. Preserve that final core of restraint. It implies reserve power and feelings that could yet be tapped, but must not be, if only to leave the audience hungry for more.

All these things require imagination and experience. Together they produce that sensitivity to musical values that makes for good interpretation. Imagination is a problem in itself. Over and over the teacher meets with the capable student who turns out one "nice" performance after another, with everything in place and all instructions followed to a T. All that his performance lacks is the spark of re-creative originality that will bring it to life. Sometimes the student can stimulate this himself by reading the music away from the piano, in complete quiet, and momentarily freed of playing notes. Then he may very well discover a swing or a drive in the rhythm that he had missed, for such innocuous performances usually have an arrhythmic foundation.

Sometimes the teacher can stimulate the student's imagination by his own performance, or by the use of meaningful adjectives such as sinister, ecstatic, portentous, frisky, serene, doleful. Indeed, this has always been a favorite means by which composers describe their intentions, from Frescobaldi to Scriabin. Often artist recordings will provide the necessary stimulus, although their continued use as models for performance tends to atrophy rather than nourish the imagination. Probably the opposite procedure is more constructive, in which the student makes his own recordings in order to get an objective hearing of his artistic shortcomings. In the main, however, the teacher can go only so far, after which the student will have to light his own inspirational fires.

PRACTICE METHODS THAT SAVE TIME AND EFFORT

The quotation from Bacon at the head of this book is now commended to the reader who may weary of being told so often, in simpler English, that we learn exactly what we practice. Three statements to this effect, thus far, are perhaps too many. Yet the principle, being a basic one, cannot help but reappear. It certainly should be ever welcome to the many would-be pianists who feel they are wasting time in practice. And that brings us to the text of the immediate discussion, which is efficiency in practice methods.

When Bacon wrote, ". . . if they be not well advised, [men] do exercise their faults and get ill habits as well as good," he could just as well have been referring to accuracy in piano practice. For, in brief, the pianist who makes mistakes in his practice learns them whether he means to or not. The viciousness of this fact may not be immediately apparent. To state it more fully, the pianist who makes a slip, chalks it up to carelessness or to human error, or he merely calls it an accident. But the

learning process does not distinguish between accidents and conscious efforts. Whatever is done is learned and becomes a muscular co-ordination. Mistakes become learned and stick just as correct procedures do. In fact, old mistakes, although they are subsequently corrected with great care, have a demonic way of turning up in public performance.

Every teacher knows the student who makes so many mistakes in his playing that he figuratively stutters at the piano, and he knows that the habit can be just about as hard to cure as stuttering. I remember a young lady in a conservatory who practiced doggedly, day in and day out, for several months, at Bach's Two-Part Invention in F minor. I began to listen to her when I noticed how every measure was peppered with trials and errors before the right notes appeared. Presently I realized that this was extremely successful practice, if not from the young lady's or Bach's standpoint, at least from the standpoint of muscular co-ordination; for every mistake that had once been an accident was now a well-learned, thoroughly mastered, integral part of the piece, a part that could be counted on with certainty to appear each time the piece was repeated!

But, the student will argue, accidents are accidents, so what can I do? And the answer? You can do a great deal if you set your mind to it. Mainly you can catch yourself before you make the mistake, just as you would if you found yourself about to walk off a cliff or to run down a pedestrian. The fact must be granted, however, that catching oneself or anticipating the mistake in advance can be very difficult. The student who has fallen into the mistake habit is usually the type whom the momentum of the rhythm leads around by the nose. Once on the verge of a mistake, the rhythmic drive pushes him over, and he realizes his error too late. Too late, because even going back to correct the mistake does little toward counteracting the muscular co-ordination that has been practiced.

The cure for this habit often takes patience and time. First, the student must establish as his motto the words *Hesitate rather than err.* He should understand that mistakes stick, but hesitations of thought are easily bridged over in due time. They are, in fact, a normal characteristic in the early stages of any learning. Second, a corrective should be instituted, a corrective more painful to the student than the disturbance caused by his mistakes. One effective device, though certainly inefficient as a practice method, is to begin a piece and start over every time the slightest slip of any sort is made, even the kind that is truly a "human error." After one gets almost to the end several times, and if the patience of student and teacher are not yet exhausted, the desire to get through the piece will usually overcome the momentum factor and bring home the value of hesitating rather than erring. The student will be helped, too, by actually hearing and seeing the teacher's demonstration of careful, cautious practice.

If the student *is* too late, and the mistake has already been "learned," then he may try an interesting corrective recommended by psychologists and typists: Their remedy is to go back and make the mistake deliberately a time or two, the theory being that making an error consciously will rid it of its involuntary character by bringing it to the surface (that is, into the consciousness). Neither teacher nor student should encircle the mistake with a pencil. (One soon learns to recognize the age of such mistakes, like the age of trees, by the number of rings.) This merely encourages the student *not* to be careful about what is *not* so marked! In summary, we can see the importance of intelligent concentration as against the "brute force" method of constant repetition, whose only advantage is that it does not tax the weary mind.

Learning is thought to represent the combining of a series of individual reflexes into one continuous or chain reflex, with each individual reflex setting off the next one. This leads to the question, often argued, as to whether it is better to practice from the whole to its parts, or vice versa. Without attempting a general answer, I may say that in my own experience it is usually better to start by practicing the entire piece or movement and including everything at once, from fingering to dynamics, always remembering the value of hesitation as a means of insuring accuracy. The hesitation permits the student to think through one thing at a time before doing everything at once.

The student may complain that there is too much to do at once, but, again, if he does *not* do everything at once he is likely to practice incorrectly what he misses. Then he will be at still greater pains to unlearn and relearn these neglects later on. One cannot say, "Today I shall learn the notes, tomorrow the fingering, and the next day the dynamics," as though adding story upon story to the foundation of a house. If the student needs an intermediate stage, the right answer is one-hand practice, which, in any case, should be a regular stage in his mastery of a new piece.

By going right through the piece from the start, the student will find that many easier problems take care of themselves in the course of several playings, leaving relatively few sections to be practiced separately as the piece nears completion. Small-section practice should serve largely as a means of final polishing. He who begins by trying to perfect the first line, then the next, and so on, usually ends up with the beginning sounding fine, the middle fair, and the ending weak, to say the least. If anything, the ending should sound best, since it leaves the last impression. By practicing the entire piece, beginning on page 3 on Tuesday if page 2 marked the end of Monday's practice, the effort will be evenly distributed.

After making some headway, the student is tempted to practice fast all the time. The danger here, however, is that the larger, chain reflex will begin to disintegrate if the individual reflexes are not continually renewed by slow practice. That is, after practicing only fast for a while, the student is surprised to find his piece falling apart instead of improving. Too much emphasis can hardly be placed on the need for slow practice as a means of concentrating *consciously* on the notes. It is by getting time to think them through that one both makes and restores the individual reflexes. Slow practice also permits free, exaggerated muscular action by whichever mechanisms are doing the playing, this being another means of restoring the individual reflexes, although a means that must not be allowed to induce tightness. A safe rule to follow is three times of slow to every two times of fast playing. Sometimes the temptation to play fast is so strong that the metronome must be used to hold down the tempo.

Of course, fast practice must not be ruled out. It is not only the way that the pianist will have to play his piece but it is the best way to eliminate waste motion (see page 44). Such motion is the bane of high speed, as I can well remember in my prancing struggles to attain speeds that my teacher seemed to play effortlessly, as though he were just coasting. Some difficulties show up only at full speed. For example, only when playing Chopin's whirlwind Prelude No. 16 in B-flat minor up to tempo does the pianist discover the prime difficulty. This lies not in the right-hand sixteenth notes but in the follow-through motion required to play the three-note left-hand groups all in one sweep. Often it is not the student's technique so much as his imagination that limits his speed. He cannot conceive the larger swing of the more rapid tempo. Then something must be done to "raise his sights." He may try letting the metronome pull him up to the fast tempo, or he may listen to a performance of the piece at that tempo.

Again, practice *what* and *only what* is needed. As the piece progresses certain parts will prove to be much easier than others. In spite of the student's temptation to play the parts he knows best, there is no point in practicing these every time the piece is played. Note how efficiently a successful conductor rehearses his orchestra. Since the professional rehearsal time is always expensive and brief, the conductor comes to the stand at the starting minute, taps for attention, and calls, "Gentlemen, start at letter O in the overture." He knows the men have played the music, that they will remember most of it readily, and that the chief trouble may occur at letter O.

If the pianist is maintaining a program of scales and other drills, he does best to distribute these throughout his practicing where they will apply to specific pieces rather than to exhaust himself by doing them all at once. The pianist will also do well to budget not only his daily time but the weeks and months that lie ahead. Experience will show him what he can expect of himself. By making a long-range schedule he will have continual goals by which he can keep tab on his progress. Some pieces take much longer to mature than others, but this fact does not impose a moral obligation on the learner to live with every piece for months or even years before he plays it. Ravel's difficult *Tzigane* was reportedly played with splendid effect for the first time by a violinist who had mastered it in exactly three days! Too often protracted study means inefficient study.

Sometimes the procrastinative student can help himself by submitting to his teacher a weekly written report of his practice and accomplishments. The teacher will also help by writing the student's assignment each week, along with specific criticisms, in a lesson notebook. In this way, the student finds himself "legally responsible" for the suggestions he has received. Even so, he had better review his lesson soon after he leaves the teacher in order to fix the many detailed suggestions that cannot be written down. Whatever his method, the student should realize that he is engaged in a kind of tortoise-versus-hare race with himself. His chances of winning out are far greater if he runs the careful, cautious course. If he is too tired or preoccupied to practice accurately when practice time comes around, then— even though this is a risky prerogative to offer the irresponsible student—he had better wait until he is thoroughly awake and able to concentrate. It is much harder to unlearn and relearn a piece that has been practiced carelessly than to begin it for the first time.

IS MEMORY YOUR UNDOING?

Memorizing might properly have been included among the practice methods just discussed. It earns this niche all by itself, however, because it ranks among the pianist's chief concerns. About a fourth of those who get ahead in piano playing have very little trouble with memorizing. For the others, this skill— and it is indeed a skill—looms as one of the biggest obstacles to their prospects of being a "compleat" pianist. "If only I didn't have to play by heart!" or "I can manage the other things but I simply can't memorize my music!" These phrases must have a familiar ring to every teacher. Why, then, do we bother to memorize? Is memorizing just an affectation made mandatory by tradition? Affectation was the word used by some of Liszt's critics when he started to give public recitals from memory; it also has been used in reference to an increasing tendency among present-day orchestra leaders to conduct from memory. No, an element

of affectation may sometimes be present, as is the factor of tradition, but there are much better reasons for memorizing.

From the student's standpoint, memorizing is the best means of insuring that the notes get from the printed page into himself. It is second only to the fingering he works out as a way of compelling careful attention to detail. While perfect memorizing is no proof positive of complete understanding, it is at least evidence that all the minutiae have been perceived and recorded.

From the performer's standpoint, it is often a technical necessity. The success of certain blind pianists notwithstanding, most of us still need to eye the keyboard in the livelier passages, leaving little time to read a score. Liszt was hardly the first performer to play from memory, but one can understand from the wide leaps and extended range of his music why he found this necessary.

Finally, memorizing is an undeniable advantage as well as a convenience to artistic playing. The elimination of note reading and page turning allows the performer to devote just that much more attention to his performance. It also permits the music to be called forth from inside oneself, as it were, so that the notes are assimilated before rather than while they are performed. One may argue that the fear of forgetting is at least as much of a distraction as page turning and note reading. The only answer is that if the piece is thoroughly memorized there will not be such a fear. One may also argue that most chamber music players still perform in public with their notes. This is true, but the string and wind players do not need to watch their finger boards or keys, and the pianist has other reasons for needing the music in front of him. He watches the full chamber music score. Besides, the fact is that experienced performers of chamber music often find themselves playing for stretches at a time without a glance at their music.

It is well known that several kinds of memory contribute to secure memorization—among them auditory, visual, touch, and intellectual memory. In actual practice what do these mean? Auditory memory is the kind that enables us to hear what comes next in the music. Most performers have no difficulty remembering the approaching sound as they play along. But many of them cannot translate this into fingers and keys when they hit a snag. In other words—and this goes back to the first topic in this book—these persons cannot play by ear. They are the ones who tend to stop cold when something throws them off ("I don't know what happened; everything just seemed to go blank!"). By contrast, the performer who plays by ear can usually get near enough to the actual notes he hears to improvise his way out of his troubles, or at least to improvise to a respectable cadence from which he can either go on or go back.

Visual memory is the kind that leaves us a mental image of the way the notes look on the printed page, or, more commonly, the way they look on the keyboard. This kind undoubtedly helps, but there is not much the student can do to further it. Any time spent trying to recall the look of the staff or the keyboard is probably much better spent on other, more positive, approaches to memorizing.

Touch memory is the sort that allows us to play the piece by muscular feel and momentum. In other words, it is habit. It plays an important part in the automatic quality of continuous playing from memory, as does hearing. The habit on which touch memory depends is muscular co-ordination. Muscular co-ordination will be very secure if the music has been practiced accurately, sufficiently, and with the same fingering. Otherwise it will be insecure, with the chances for successful memorizing affected accordingly. Yet, at best, touch memory alone does not suffice for secure memorizing. The moment a slip occurs to throw the performer off the automatic track, he is lost—just as is the novice salesman who is interrupted in his prepared talk. Then other types of memory must be called to assistance.

Intellectual memory is the kind that results from a knowledge of the music. It is the kind with which the performer can do most on short notice and without which he will never feel secure. Anything that brings the music to the performer's consciousness contributes to intellectual memory, whether it concerns form, tonality, counting, technique, melodic line, or programmatic suggestion. If he is observant when he practices he will mentally record much about the music that will stand him in good stead.

This much is relatively painless. But most players will do well to face the fact with courage—for courage is what deliberate memorizing takes—that a certain amount of ornery, tedious work is required to assimilate this knowledge. Such memorizing of the music must make sense to the performer. He must see the details in intelligible groups and patterns. He must train himself to look ahead to the next division in the form. A succession of dominants, a chord built in fourths, a series of three-measure phrases, a bass line that descends by twos, a rondo design, a canonic progression—all of these are dependable aids to him who discovers them.

Memorizing is discussed last in this chapter on practice methods only because the other topics need to be considered first in learning a new piece. However, that does not mean that memorizing should be delayed until late in the development of a piece. The teacher who waits until the student can play the piece nearly perfectly to say, "All right, now go memorize it," is almost asking the student to relearn the piece. Of course, many students will have just about memorized the piece by this time, anyway, but the others will find that playing from memory is a very different experience from playing with the score before them. Memorizing is certainly a skill in its own right. Therefore, it must be practiced just like any other skill if there is to be any hope of relying on it in performance. The student should begin to play from memory as soon as the habits of fingering, counting, and interpretation are correctly planted. Even before this time some players like to memorize the technically most difficult passages as a means of speeding up their practice.

To go about memorizing, the student's first rule is to dispense with the music once and for all, except for necessary reference. Curiously, the habits of looking at the score and playing from memory fight each other. Not only may memorizing seem difficult when one is used to looking at the score, but, conversely, reading from the score becomes difficult after one gets used to playing from memory! In fact, students often note that they undo their hard-earned memorizing by returning to the score for a time. Going back to crutches is no way to get rid of them.

Dispensing with the music does not mean leaving the music on the rack and merely averting the eyes from it. There is too great a temptation or unconscious inclination to peek. Much better is to put the music on top of the upright piano or far enough back on the grand piano that the student has to stand to refer to it. Then he tries harder to recall the note. A note recalled with such effort is a note won by the memory. (My memorizing has come best when I had to do it but mislaid the score!)

The student should work on a page or more at a sitting, dividing the music into logical sections. Doing too little or too much at a time is inefficient. The amount his mind can encompass will depend on the nature of the music and will increase as his piano playing advances. Homophonic music usually takes hold quicker than contrapuntal or extremely dissonant music. When he first tries to play from memory he is likely to get stuck very soon. If he cannot recall the note he should stand to check the score, try to see the note in some sort of intelligible pattern, then resume from where he stopped, *not from the beginning*. In this way, he may have to stand twenty-five times before he completes the section. But he will be surprised the next time to find that he has to stand only, say, fifteen times. Five of those times may be to check former spots that he missed, and the others will be new ones. Eventually he may have to check nearly every note. Yet, in its plodding way, though it may tire the standing muscles, this system works, and works in a way that is fundamentally right and efficient learning.

When the student returns to his memorizing the next day, he should make certain that he begins with a new section, thus doing his hardest concentrating while he is freshest. The old material will seem easier when he gets back to it later in the practice session. An indispensable means of clinching the memory work is to count from memory. The counting keeps track of the bar line and all that that implies, both rhythmically and harmonically. Uncertain counting, like uncertain fingering, is sure to mean uncertain memorizing. Finally, the student should have landmarks every few measures at logical cadential points in the music, where he can begin anew if he does get stuck. To make certain that these landmarks can be recalled on split-second notice, at the first sign of memory failure, he should practice skipping about arbitrarily from any one to any other. And it is a good idea to try this in the mind alone, away from the piano. In fact, it is excellent preparation to go through the entire work in that way, although the feat is certainly one requiring unusual powers of concentration. In any case, the landmarks will stave off disaster until one gets to that rare point where he literally knows every note of the piece. To play from the beginning to the end of a piece without any such landmarks is about like walking a tightrope from rim to rim of the Grand Canyon.

IV. Performance

HAVING fought his way thus far along the tortuous road that leads to accomplished pianism, the student, like Tamino in *The Magic Flute*, is ready for his final test—performance. Performance requires perfection of the music and

good poise on the stage. Both the perfection and the poise present special problems, some of them interdependent, that will presently be considered. First, the recalcitrant student may want to know why he should perform at all. A comparatively few students perform because they hope to have concert careers. The others, if they ever do perform, perform because their teachers present recitals, or their parents and friends ask them to play, or they themselves welcome the chance to show what they can do.

Is the teacher justified in putting on the recitals? Yes, for three reasons: the recitals mark periodic goals toward which the student can work, they afford unusual opportunities to view the student's work in perspective, and they provide performance experience. The last reason is often given as the first, though it may well be the least important one. Too much emphasis is usually placed on the experience in public performance that the recitals will afford. Recitals, well coached, do train the student in poise before an audience, but they are no assurance that every performance will go without a hitch. Most depends on how well the music has been learned on each occasion. Even the most experienced pianists face disaster if they dare to appear without proper preparation, while a totally inexperienced student may "knock the sparks off" a piece that has been well learned.

THAT LAST MILE THAT MEANS PERFECTION

One of the most disheartening truths to face in a frank discussion of piano problems is that so many students repeatedly fall just short of satisfactory performance. Like the indomitable Admiral Peary in his first, abortive attempts to reach the North Pole, they get almost within sight of their goal and are compelled to abandon the project. They spend weeks, perhaps months, going through all the stages of fingering, counting, technical drill, interpretative analysis, and even memorizing, only to find, for one reason or another, that they cannot quite make that last mile that means perfection. What keeps them from going all the way?

The problem may be a specific one, concerned with a particular musical indiscretion; if so, with the odds brought more into his favor, the student should soon enjoy the success that ultimately crowned Admiral Peary's efforts. Or the problem may reveal more deep-seated failings, failings that will or will not submit to extensive treatment. Among specific faults, the most usual is to attempt too hard a piece. This can be the fault of the student, who is eager to get to the masterworks that he has tried over or heard in concert; or it can be the fault of the teacher, who is also eager to see his student progress and so continually overestimates his abilities.

The student may attempt a piece that is not too hard but too long—too long for his concentration span in performance and too long for thorough attention to all sections either in his practice or at the lesson. He may get the piece off to a careless start and never quite be able to undo the original errors. This is especially common when bad fingering is allowed. He may request or be given an inferior piece not worth the trouble it takes to learn, and may utterly tire of it before he works it up. Or he may leap into a modern or early idiom so foreign to the Chopin, Grieg, and Rachmaninoff on which he has so far thrived, that he simply cannot adapt himself in the space of one piece.

Among the more deep-seated reasons for not attaining perfection, defective muscianship and unusual physical clumsiness should be mentioned. These are less common than one might suppose, yet when they are present they are very unfortunate. So often they seem to afflict serious, ambitious students, the kind for whom one would wish the best in the world, but perhaps the kind whose chief trait is really love of hard discipline. That these students should be the ones is probably because any other kind of student would have been discouraged much earlier in his piano study. Typical are those who cannot memorize because they lack a musical ear, who cannot play fluently because they do not feel the rhythmic swing, who cannot surmount technical difficulties because their muscular action is unusually stiff and unyielding. Patient return to musical or technical rudiments may very well bring passable results over a period of time, especially since these are the students who are anxious to give the time.

Another deep-seated reason is chronic bad practice. Chronic bad practice differs from an occasional lapse in that it indicates an underlying inability on the student's part to apply himself regularly. In fact, it ordinarily represents a personality or adjustment problem only too familiar to every understanding teacher. It shows up most commonly in the brilliant student who goes by fits and starts, with occasional flashes of rare talent and long periods of near-hopeless meandering. By contrast, we may compare the more "normal" student who is irritatingly slower in his responses, yet, in the end, somehow manages to turn out one "bang up" performance after another.

To be sure, the teacher should not expect, or rather, ought not presume, to be a psychiatrist. However, he knows that the very nature of music is likely to attract sensitive persons with their share of the common neuroses and anxieties; and that the highly exacting requirements of performance, in which the utmost concentration is required and only a fraction of an inch separates accuracy from error, is likely to bring these traits forward. Therefore, if he is a mature and sympathetic person, he may at least recognize the symptoms and bear them in mind, perhaps even call them to the student's attention if that can be tactfully accomplished without making him feel that he is a "mental case."

The teacher will understand, in any event, that the old complaint, "He has oodles of talent but is simply too lazy to practice!" hardly tells the whole or even the correct story. A physically healthy person who seems outstandingly lazy or careless is very often in actuality a person who is blocked from the effort and patient concentration he himself would like to give by some emotional maladjustment. What that maladjustment may be is of course out of the province of the student or teacher to judge. But simply bringing out the general nature of the problem as it affects piano playing and merely removing the stigma of the word *lazy* often help the student to bring in better and more consistent results.

The evidences of some sort of maladjustment will be recognized by student and teacher alike. There is the "fair weather" pianist who practices when everything is just right, which means that most of the time he must beg off or miss lessons with a remarkable assortment of excuses. He is the one who promises to have a much better lesson next time and to institute a permanent reform thereafter. Also he is the one who, in the more advanced types, somehow gets a sprained finger or wrenched shoulder just before he is scheduled to play somewhere. "Accident-prone," the psychoanalysts call it.

Then there is the pianist who always wants a different piece or a different teacher. He complains that he did not get off to a good start or defeatedly berates himself for a bad start, hoping to do much better if he is given a new lease on life. And there is the pianist who shows an almost morbid dread of public performance, chiefly because he takes himself much too seriously. These types and many others sometimes go on for years without conspicuous progress, yet without dropping out, because they love music and in their own ways realize that they have unmistakable talent.

Now, for the "average" or "normal" student, a few suggestions may be given for polishing music that is still short of the performance level. If persistent hitches continue to plague the music, the pianist should first of all look for wrong fingering, uncertain counting, excessive fast practice, or a basic fault in technical method. To make as near certain as human beings can that he has uncovered all the potential hitches in performance, he should try the device of shutting his eyes and counting aloud from memory with the metronome set at a slow tempo. Wherever his fingers or the counting falter he will know that he needs extra practice.

This device is also an excellent means of maintaining conscious memory of the music—that is, of keeping the memorizing from becoming entirely automatic. As we have seen, memorizing that becomes entirely automatic leaves the performer stranded the moment something interrupts the playing sequence. He tells himself that he played the piece perfectly beforehand and wonders why he gets stuck now, not realizing that the very different circumstances of actual performance nullify the automatic memory by causing him to note consciously what he is doing.

All pieces should be accurately timed in advance to avoid the embarrassment of too-skimpy or too-lengthy a program. Frequent timing also helps to keep tab on one's progress. After a piece is brought to performance level, it proves almost as hard to keep at that level as it was to learn. Like the boxer before a fight, one can easily overtrain. Until the day of the program, the piece needs to be kept in cold storage, so to speak, halfway between the evils of neglect and overpractice. I usually recommend that my students play such pieces through once daily, followed only by what practice proves to be needed on that day.

The period of "cold•storage" should be a period of technical and artistic maturation. Therein lies a principal reason for maintaining a repertoire, another being that all of our friends are "from Missouri" and insist on being shown just what can be played. Artistic maturation is certainly a better reason for a repertoire than some such fear as that one day a conductor will unwittingly switch concertos on us at the last moment (as seems to have happened to almost every pianist who has written memoirs, not to mention the countless occasions on which "I did not see the score of the music until it was handed to me on the train en route to the concert").

The student should make a special point of playing right through the piece or program he hopes to present without a stop, under conditions as near to actual performance as can be attained, once every day for at least two weeks or a month before the planned date. Otherwise he will be dismayed to learn, as amateur choral and orchestral conductors so often are, that the all-important factors of continuity and perspective are lost when the music is picked apart right up to the last minute. And in some pieces (such as the Chopin Etudes) only now will he learn that a real problem of muscular endurance exists, calling for changes that will minimize motions and husband the strength. The playing-through might well be the first thing done each day. A "cold" performance is about as handicapped as a nervous one. To critical ears it becomes a fair measure both of how ready a piece is and what spots will need most practice that day. It can be still more realistic if one imagines the recital atmosphere, complete even to a sample case of nerves and all the motions from walking on the stage to bowing and walking off again.

Shortly before the day of performance the student should go through several dress rehearsals (or "dry runs," as the Army terms them), calling in a few obliging friends at a time. Their criticisms may do a lot to put final touches on the playing. As the music reaches its last stages of polishing, the student will notice that the problem of concentration comes more and more to the fore. Not only does he have to fight completely automatic memory but he finds that just the act of keeping his mind on what he is doing without letup, especially in a full-length suite or sonata, is difficult. The pianist is rhythmically bound to keep going without a break from the beginning to the end of a piece or movement. Unlike the actor, who is much less rigidly bound to tempo and has at least some relaxation during the other actors' lines to be recalling his own, the pianist has only the breathing spaces that his music permits. And those breathing spaces he must make the most of. Daily performancese *without stops* gradually help him to locate slight rest spots, as necessary for the sound as they are for the playing, to relax where there was tension, and to get deeper and deeper into the spirit of the music itself.

THE WORST BOGEY OF THEM ALL—STAGE FRIGHT

Finally, we reach the problem of stage fright, which, whether they will confess it or not, is the worst bogey of all for most performers. No cure has been found that wholly eliminates stage fright, but there are certain facts, attitudes, and procedures that can do a great deal toward alleviating it. These may be introduced point by point.

Nearly everybody gets stage fright. Virtually all performers from beginners to top concert artists experience stage fright. In a recent article, Vladimir Horowitz acknowledged that to this day he still gets "butterflies" before every concert. Students who feel that they are exceptional in being bothered by stage fright should take note.

Being realistic about it helps. If the pianist faces the fact that he will undergo a certain amount of fear when he performs he will actually reduce that fear somewhat. This he will do, paradoxically, by removing the disturbing uncertainty as to whether he will be troubled by stage fright. The Army recognized the value of that approach when it prepared the men going into battle with, "Naturally you'll be afraid. Who wouldn't be?"

Hiding the fact fools nobody. The pianist who tries to avoid the thought beforehand or tries to tell himself that stage fright does not exist is in for a rude awakening. I knew a fine young lady pianist who sought to divert her mind from the fear of playing before an audience by reading Shakespeare just before each concert. The result was that she usually walked on the stage with excellent composure and almost collapsed in the first few minutes as the reality of the situation forced itself upon her.

Going to the other extreme can also do harm. Of course, there is always the danger that the realist will exaggerate the problem in his eagerness to recognize it. Then, ironically, he will be defeating the very purpose of his realism. He will no doubt appear on the platform with a scared and harassed expression that will immediately be taken up by the audience, for the performer's demeanor is highly contagious. The moral of this observation is to look proud no matter what happens. If one makes a frightful slip he must behave like the chess player who wears that just-what-I-had-in-mind look when he discovers he has left his queen *en prise.*

Public performance should be seen in perspective. The performer is right in taking his music seriously and giving his very best when he performs. But he must not take himself too seriously. He needs to remember how it feels to be on the audience side. Some of that mysterious public, that expressionless, unknown group, will really appreciate and value what he does well. Others will undoubtedly yawn and keep tugging at their watches, and there may even be a few who have come to backbite over the least flaw. But that is as it is at all concerts. After all, ninety-nine years from now it will not matter too much how the concert went or what the people thought.

Confidence means knowing the music. The performer who

is genuinely confident of himself is the one who is genuinely convinced that he has mastered the music. If there are any misgivings in his mind regarding fingering, counting, technique, memory, interpretation, or other essentials, then he has cause for real fear, not just bogey fear. This point can hardly be over-emphasized. The performer may not even be willing to admit this to himself, but wherever there are shaky passages that result from slipshod or insufficient practice and lack of patience with detail, those spots are certain to cause anxiety. Every pianist who has played in public at all knows with what different degrees of confidence he embarks on an old tried-and-true war horse whose success has been assured by many past performances as compared with a new, untested composition. This fact leads to the related one that

Confidence grows with each successful performance of a piece and diminishes with each failure. The main lesson to learn from this principle is that a piece played without reasonable assurance of success, because of inadequate practice or unfavorable circumstances, may be that much harder to play the next time.

Nervousness should be taken into consideration in practicing. In keeping with the idea of being realistic about stage fright, the student should practice each passage with the thought that his fingers may very well be jittery when they play it. In other words, he should make allowance for nervousness, which is the product of stage fright, by learning the passage just that much better than would be necessary if he were not nervous. Correct use of the fingers and hand and the covering of as many of the coming keys as possible in "position" technique (discussed earlier) help to counteract finger nervousness. Some pianists feel that they are at their best only when they are a little nervous. Their nervousness is "sublimated" into increased energy and sensitivity at the time of performance.

Good physical condition is a kind of antitoxin for nervousness.

The performer who is free of colds, unusual pains, outside worries, and fatigue is in a much better position to meet stage fright than the one who is not. By sufficient sleep and healthy living he builds up resistance to the fear of playing. Moreover, he puts himself in the proper frame of mind for the intense concentration that performance requires. It is the highly enervating strain of such concentration and not the physical exertion that leads to nervous exhaustion after a concert. Furthermore, healthy living, including outdoor recreation, lends a robust glow and artistic virility to the playing that seem to counteract fear just as "hothouse pallor" seems to beget it.

Adequate rest just before the performance is especially important. The performer who has not readied himself far enough in advance will find that last-minute cramming is hardly conducive to self-confidence. It wears him out, fails to "take," confuses what he has already done, and in general makes him anxious. Most pianists develop their own preconcert routines, planned so as to allow them some rest. I myself like to be "well slept" before the day of a concert. Early in the day I prefer merely to "walk" through the program, then avoid undue strain in the day's affairs, eat a very light supper, sleep for an hour, and warm up carefully and easily on scales and other drills a half hour before concert time.

The anticipation of attendant details prevents distressing upsets. Perhaps "details" is not quite the right word for the bow tie that loses itself or the E-flat that sticks just before concert time. Such things can terrify a pianist who discovers them just as he is all set to go. Yet the fault is his for not looking after these things ahead of time. Experienced pianists do not trust to chance but plan ahead. They never assume that the piano will have been tuned, or the keys washed, or the programs proofread, or the publicity handled, or the lighting set, or the proper bench provided, or suitable practice time scheduled where the performance is to be given. A checklist of all possible contingencies is a wise precaution.

Proper warming-up gets the program off to a reassuring start. Pianists dread the cold, clammy hands that characteristically go with stage fright. Sometimes, in spite of the most thorough warm-up drills, the hands remain chilled and unresponsive. I should like to recommend the use of a few easy calisthenics and body-stretching exercises just before going on stage. These get the blood into circulation and warm not only the hands but the whole body. Besides, limbering of this sort provides the muscle "tone" necessary for athletic technical requirements. A deliberate reminder to oneself to breathe steadily is also helpful. This may be necessary to counteract a natural tendency to hold the breath when nervous, which in turn unsteadies the muscles by reducing the oxygen content in the blood.

Learning from one's failures does not mean giving up in despair. Finally, just this word of caution. The performer who gives a bad recital must not let that scare him out of ever giving another. There is no honest performer who will not confess to at least one bad recital somewhere in his history. A bad recital can be highly instructive in a graphic way. The performer must learn, as the bridge player does, that he has to lose a good many times in a good many ways in order to become a consistent winner.

V. Nine Steps in Learning
a New Piece

IN THESE last two chapters the emphasis is on the pianist's problems of learning and teaching—on "methodology," to use the more awesome term. The particular aim of the present chapter is to propose a plan for learning a new piece. This plan comes best this late in the book because it provides good opportunities to bring together the main points made in earlier chapters and to illustrate them in specific, practical situations.

How to start a new piece and what then to do are major concerns of every piano student. If he has no "route map," as it were, he may get the general direction but is likely to lose time, get discouraged, or even give up in despair. What he needs is a series of steppingstones that reduce his journey to shorter, more obvious hops, somewhat as described on pages 3 to 4. No wonder *Gradus ad Parnassum* has been such a favorite title in any sort of instruction book.

The teacher needs a sequence of procedures to follow in teaching the new piece, too. One sure sign of an inexperienced teacher is the lack of just such procedures. This lack is perhaps more familiar when the problem is to correct faulty playing. In the manner of a good doctor, the good teacher must be able not only to diagnose bad playing, but to prescribe the remedies that will cure it.

The procedures demonstrated here are recommended for any pianist who has passed the more elementary stages of playing and is ready, say, for his first Bach Invention. They are not generally recommended, nor is any other inductive method, for beginners, who can get off to a much better start, in my opinion, by taking the sight-reading approach described in the final chapter. The illustrations used in this chapter are taken from somewhat more advanced pieces so as to include a wider range of learning problems.

By way of a "route map," an outline of nine steps to be taken in learning the new piece is offered here. This outline derives from the problems listed under Practice on page 74 and from a subdivision of the three phases of learning by which this chapter is organized. In the discussions that follow, most attention is paid to the earlier of the nine steps, these being the steps on which a good foundation depends and the ones that call for the most specific illustrations. But in actual practicing the three phases take about equal time, or an average of two to six weeks each, depending not only on the length and difficulty of the piece but on the method of practice (see pages 109–110).

OUTLINE FOR LEARNING A NEW PIECE

Phase I. Laying the Groundwork
    Step 1. Choosing the piece (balanced diet, quality, length, technical level, and edition)
    Step 2. Understanding the piece (first readings and analysis)
    Step 3. Planning the ways and means (markings, touches, and fingering)
Phase II. Learning the Notes
    Step 4. Fixing the habits and co-ordinations
    Step 5. Counting with the metronome at a slow tempo
    Step 6. Memorizing (patterns and relationships; more counting with the metronome)
Phase III. Playing the Music
    Step 7. Counting with metronome up to tempo

Step 8. Polishing in small-section practice (exercises, touches, pedaling, and tone production)

Step 9. Interpreting the piece as a whole (phrasing, markings, climaxes, continuity, and time to mature)

STEPS 1 TO 3: LAYING THE GROUNDWORK

Choosing the piece. The student should be invited to suggest his own choice for a new piece. Too often he is simply assigned the piece, with no questions asked. And too often it will be limited to one of those tried-and-true but shopworn successes that define a too-narrow pedagogic rut. With the richest of all music repertoires to choose from, the pianist's horizons can and should be much wider. Naturally, the student who has access to a basic library of piano music and does daily, planned sight reading in it will know best what he wants.

The choice will depend in part on particular needs. I am not thinking so much of meeting specific technical needs—for instance, choosing a piece because it should strengthen the weak fifth finger. As we have seen, that familiar sort of reasoning puts the cart before the horse. One does better to choose a piece for its musical value, then work on the fifth finger as it may prove inadequate for that piece. But I do mean that the student who hopes to be well rounded in the field has a need to live with at least each main composer listed in our Basic Library, and to be at home in the styles and forms of each of the four main eras of keyboard music:

THE FOUR MAIN ERAS OF KEYBOARD MUSIC

Baroque Era, about 1580–1750. Byrd, Bull, Gibbons, and Purcell in England; Frescobaldi and Domenico Scarlatti in Italy; Couperin and Rameau in France; and Bach and Handel in Germany. Age of the harpsichord and clavichord, of motivic writing in more or less polyphonic texture, and of certain options in performance (as in the ornaments). Fugues, suites of dances, variations, and freer types such as preludes and programme pieces.

Classic Era, about 1730–1830. Haydn, Mozart, and Beethoven in Vienna; also, lesser pianist-composers like Clementi and Hummel. Rise of the "pianoforte"; age of more phrasewise writing, the Alberti bass, "singing-allegro," and other more homophonic styles. Chiefly sonatas, concertos, duets, variations, rondos, and fantasias.

Romantic Era, about 1790–1910. Schubert, Mendelssohn, Schumann, Chopin, Liszt, Brahms, Grieg, Fauré, MacDowell, and Rachmaninoff. The age of the piano, now enlarged and perfected in its action, pedals, frame, etc.; also, virtuoso playing, chromatic harmony, homophony, the um-pah-pah bass, idiomatic keyboard figures, and expression ranging from intimate and poetic to grandiose and bombastic. Programme and character pieces, rhapsodies, fantasy sonatas and concertos, two-piano works, and etudes.

Modern Era, about 1890 to the present. Debussy, Ravel, and Milhaud in France; Hindemith in Germany; Bartok in Hungary; Scriabin and Prokofiev in Russia; and Bloch and Copland in America. Age of experiments in harmony, tonality, and sonority; percussive touches; return to motivic and polyphonic writing; and complex meters. Forms mainly from the past (as in Neo-Classicism).

Unless students are invited into the other three eras they tend to choose little else but Romantic pieces. They need a more balanced diet, even among the pieces under way at any one time. Every so often, too, they will want an ensemble piece, as urged in our first chapter; or a "concert arrangement," as of a folk song, or an organ chorale prelude. The many transcriptions

Bach himself made are good enough precedent for the use of arrangements. The criterion is the taste with which they are made.

Of course, the quality of the piece chosen, whether original or arranged, cannot be graded by any fixed standards—not while music is an art. The safest way to know good from bad is to grant that the mainstream of keyboard music is time- and audience-proven. It is what any student should be bred on first, anyway, always remembering that the mainstream includes many things besides the most hackneyed pieces. Later he will have the judgment to choose from less-known works. Fortunately, most of the great masters from Bach to Bartok left easier pieces too. These might legitimately be called "teaching pieces." Otherwise, one cannot help suspecting much of that large quantity of pedagogic material on the music dealers' shelves. Too much of it has been written by successful, well-meaning teachers who forget that unless they have also had bona fide training in composition they ought to stick pretty much to teaching, leaving the composers to do the composing! Such material is not improved, either, by the glittering, often very enticing covers in which it is now dressed. A nice cover has a psychological advantage if it is not exploited to hide a shoddy interior. But good music will sell itself. It needs no come-ons, apologies, stunts, or other special inducements.

Other factors in the choice of a new piece are its length and its difficulty (athletic or otherwise), and the matter of a good edition. These were considered on pages 118–119, 32, 27–31, and 77.

Understanding the music. The learning of a new piece becomes much more effective when the pianist tries first to understand its meaning and form. A survey of musical form is beyond the limits of this book (reference is made again to *Understanding Music* in the Source References), but at least a method of approach can be illustrated here. As in all steps of the learning, the student must do the work himself as far as possible (see page 73).

Bach's fugues offer as much of a learning and teaching challenge as anything in the standard literature. Harder to explain than to hear, they run on in a braidlike texture that must be unraveled yet does not divide into clearly contrasted sections as do the ABA and like forms of Classic and Romantic pieces. Similar problems occur, if to a lesser extent, in Bach's Inventions and suite movements. Therefore, for our main illustrations one complete fugue is copied in Ex. 24 from the Bach-Gesellschaft *Urtext* edition of *The Well-Tempered Clavier*, Book 1.

Would that every editor and publisher might insert measure numbers as in Ex. 24. These are a real convenience, not only in this sort of analysis but at the lesson or in a contest, where the teacher or judge can refer to them in remarks jotted down rapidly during a performance. They also permit the teacher to sit at another piano and make references from his own score without getting up each time to point out the measure. When the numbers must be written in, as is usually true, a good way is to indicate just the first measure in each brace with a heavy figure encircled at the left. (See Ex. 25.) Upbeat measures at the start are not included; nor is an optional ending or a part of a measure after a repeat bar. Separate movements are numbered separately.

To start off, if the student reads reasonably well he should read right through the new piece a few times, as musically as possible. The purpose is to get some idea of it as a whole and what the work will entail, without going too far by letting any faults take root. A time or two through with a good recording and the score is a help, too, if one bears in mind the danger of getting overly dependent on the recording (page 104).

To begin the analysis and be able, later, to keep track of the separate lines or "voices," play each line alone from start to finish. Better still, sing and conduct it in any convenient range,

Ex. 24

using letter names (see page 10). It helps to label each voice according to its range (S., A., T., or B.) as is done in Ex. 24 at the first entries and after each prolonged rest. Dotted lines help to keep track of shifts between staffs, as in measure 10. These shifts and the confusion of upstem and downstem notes on two staffs make the lines harder to disentangle in fugues of more voices (for instance, at measures 85 to 87 of the C-sharp minor Fugue in the same collection).

While the lines are being read separately the main ideas should be identified so that they can eventually be made to stand out in the texture if and as desired. Each entry of the subject can be marked by some symbol, usually a pair of diagonal lines, as at the fourteen entries marked in our F major Fugue. Any standard contrapuntal devices can be observed at this time, such as the strettos at the octave in measures 36 to 40 and 46 to 51. The example we have taken has no augmentations or diminutions but does include "false entries" (as in the tenor at measures 7 to 9), a decorated entry in the soprano (measures 64 to 68), and hints of inversion (as in the bass of measures 55 to 56), none of which is likely to be mere "happenstance" in Bach. Any other recurring ideas can now be observed, too, like the countersubject (C.S.) stated by the tenor in measures 4 to 8. The characteristic pedal point in measures 36 to 40 is still another device that needs to be kept "in view" in performance. As can be seen, what to do with spare time is one of the few problems the performer of Bach does not have.

Next, the main cadences in the course of the fugue should be labeled according to key, as at measures 45 to 46 and 55 to 56. Most Bach fugues average two to five internal cadences on any or all of the nearest related keys. These are the main landmarks of fugal form, often marking the goal of a modulatory episode and the re-entry of the subject in the new key. As such, they make the best points for a shift in "terrace" dynamics (page 94) and for tasteful ritards in the flow, followed by an *a tempo* (as suggested in Ex. 24). They are also useful landmarks for memorizing.

How does one spot these main cadences? For one thing, the new key is seldom if ever more than one degree away in the circle of fifths. For another, both the V and I chords are usually in root position. Third, the bass typically repeats on the fifth step (measure 55) or makes an octave leap (measure 45) before going to the new tonic. Fourth, the I chord will not be "troubled" by any dissonant tone suspended from the V chord. And last, as noted, the cadence often leads to a re-entry of the subject. Thus, measures 30 to 31 do not qualify as a main cadence since four of these six clues do not apply.

Planning the ways and means. We have looked over our route map but have yet to decide the exact roads we will be taking. Before the practicing itself can begin, we need to arrive at the styles, touches, and fingering to be used. Otherwise, as we have seen (pages 104 to 107), we would surely have to retrace many of our steps. Inasmuch as Bach, with almost no markings, poses the main problems again, let him be our point of attack once more.

Always the first problem to be decided is the prevailing tempo, since the choice of tempo must have a profound influence on all else about the music. In fact, in unedited music one should try not so much to divine the "character" in order to decide the tempo, but rather to find the tempo, which will then determine the character. There are traditional tempos for many of Bach's fugues (and actual markings or dance titles in his suite movements, of course). Today's traditions hardly go straight back to Bach's time but do deserve some respect for the accumulated musicianship they represent. For our purposes, internal evidence can be a more secure help, although there is no sure key to Bach's tempos.

Again, what are the clues? To begin, as in any piece, the tempo extremes can be set by finding the reasonable top speed at which the most difficult or awkward passages can be played, and the slowest speed at which the longest note values in the main ideas have meaning. Then one might suggest that the tempo will be slower in fugues that have, first, a thicker texture (in number of voices or closeness of imitations); second, more changes or diversions in the flow (whether rhythmic, ornamental, or technical); third, faster harmonic rhythm (ratio of harmonic changes to pulses); and fourth, a subject spread over fewer pulses (an interesting but riskier clue). Finally, there is the long held idea (dating back to the Renaissance *tactus*) that virtually all music is actually felt at a "universal" pulse rate close (and possibly related) to the heart beat—that is, around 60 to 80 on the metronome. This general pulse rate is said to operate not only when the composer specifies it by the time signature or an express marking but when he specifies twice as fast or twice as slow. Thus, Chopin uses the time signature C and the word "Presto" for his Etude in C-sharp minor, op. 10, no. 4, but the editor for the Oxford edition adds $\downarrow = 88$ rather than $\downarrow = 176$. Of course, even with a latitude of only 60 to 80, curious questions can arise. In the C minor fugue of *The Well-Tempered Clavier*, Book I, how can we prove which is the better of the two extremes, a slower than usual speed of $\downarrow = 80$ or a faster than usual speed of $\downarrow = 60$? But at least we have this way to narrow the extremes. As to whether a triple grouping is to be heard as one or three pulses, one of the extremes is usually *too* extreme to be considered.

Every one of these clues tends to confirm the general rightness of Bischoff's "Allegretto" and the compound pulse of $\downarrow. = 60$ in his edition of Ex. 24, as the reader can best discover by putting the clues to the test himself. The same clues suggest $\downarrow$ (not $\downarrow$) = 80 as a suitable tempo for the first movement of Mozart's Sonata in C minor, K. 457, the opening of which is given in Ex. 25 (after the *Urtext* in *Mozart's Werke*).

Having "captured" an approximate metronome tempo mark in writing, the student should next consider the reading or style of playing he will want to give to the main ideas and all related material in the fugue. For example, should the subject in Ex. 24 be one legato line or several groups of slurred and staccato notes? Four possibilities are suggested for measures 1 to 4. Once some such reading is decided, the remainder of the fugue would need to be worked out consistently with this reading (not done in Ex. 24). Pianists often shy away from taking this sort of initiative and seeing it through to the end. But the arguments are that the music has to be played in some manner, Bach indicated none, and it generally works better to plan that manner than to leave it mostly to intuition and chance. (This last argument raises interesting questions that must be saved for our final chapter.)

To decide a reading presupposes some feeling for historical styles. Baroque music had not yet quite the fussy niceties to be found in Classic music (see page 98). Its style in any one piece was ordinarily simpler and more uniform. Even the details specified by Mozart in Ex. 25, incomplete (and inconsistent) though they often are, might seem like overloading in Bach. It helps to realize that these styles derived, like violin bowing, from idiomatic techniques. This fact can be seen even more clearly in Domenico Scarlatti's "sonatas." Patterns of different note values, as in the subject of our fugue, fall into "natural" rhythmic and five-finger groupings. Generally, at a moderate tempo, the shorter and longer note values suggest a legato touch while eighth-notes often fall "naturally" into a staccato or portato touch (recalling the detached cello bowing commonly used for Baroque thorough-bass or "walking bass" in eighth-notes).

Ornamentation and metrically free passages should also be worked out and written down in advance rather than left to chance. These include Baroque and later signs, recitatives, *fioriture,* runs, and short cadenzas. (A student about to study a Classic concerto should get the valuable experience, too, of making up the longer cadenzas himself.) The problem is to work out rhythmic groupings of the notes, and any questions of

Ex. 25

the order and number of notes indicated by signs. Even free runs are best put into some convincing grouping for fingering, learning, and technical purposes, regardless of whether any rhythmic division is to sound through in performance. Good examples are the runs in measures 8 and 12 of the Chopin Prelude in F minor, reproduced in full in Ex. 26 (after the First Critical Edition). But it is not good, even as a teaching device, to fit the notes of a continuous trill into an exact meter, as is so often done in Bach's two-part Invention in D minor or Mozart's "easy" Sonata in C major (K. 545) at the long trills. The student who begins by measuring the trill in this fashion has a hard time *un*measuring it later. All ornaments must be treated freely and expressively.

Some basic aids for solving ornaments were offered on pages 100 to 101. But, as suggested there, serious pianists will need to seek more details for themselves, as in Putnam Aldrich's book (in the Source References) or in the few but important Baroque treatises on performance practices that have been translated (chiefly those by Couperin, Emanuel Bach, and Leopold Mozart). No student can reach pianistic adulthood without a baptism of fire in some richly ornamented piece like Bach's three-part Sinfonia in E-flat major in the embellished version or the "Sarabande" from his English Suite No. 3 in G minor. Remember that there is usually not one solution but a choice of solutions within certain limits, the problem being to find the best one for a particular context of melody, harmony, rhythm, tempo, mood, and technique.

The ornament signs that happen to occur in our Exs. 24 to 26 may be taken merely as samples of questions that are likely to arise. The trills in Ex. 24 are indicated by a wavy line (which does not mean "inverted mordent"!) or *tr.*, without any distinction intended, as is obvious here. The one in the countersubject (as in measures 7 or 30) would normally be done the same way each time. To decide exactly *what* way means reaching decisions on the usual three options (page 100). My own preference here (as noted below measure 7) would be to start on the upper tone, to trill at once and throughout the dotted quarter-note, and to end with a suffix from below. Even in a descending scale the start on the main tone is rare, chiefly when the passage is quicker or when there is a slur implying that the starting, upper tone of the trill is tied to the previous tone (as in measure 3 of the "Sarabande" mentioned before). Here, to start on the main tone calls for some way to avoid fifths. In any case, the upper tone is much the more usual starting tone and it creates the spicy dissonance that is expected of most Baroque and Classic ornaments. The "long" trill, in this instance, has the advantage of continuing the line to its goal beyond the barline. The suffix is a technical convenience. In measures 45 and 55 the cadential trills are typically "short," four-note ones, which would be inserted in this dotted cadence formula even were no sign present (as none is in measure 71).

In Mozart the principles are still much the same. The trills in Ex. 25 start on the upper note (as at the start of K. 576, too). Since Mozart has followed the frequent practice of writing in the suffix, the result is none other than a four-note turn from above, preceded in this instance by the main note as an upbeat. The actual turns in the next movement of this same Sonata are all the usual four-note type starting from above, the timing being the chief problem. In the last movement the appoggiatura comes on the beat and follows both guides given on page 101, subtracting its written value from the next note, and receiving half of that next note's value. By Chopin's time the trill was usually started on the main note, as seems best for measure 18 of Ex. 26, but more often Chopin's own music still sounds better when the old rules are applied.

Not enough is known yet about the widespread practice of "expressive rhythm" in Baroque performance to enable the average pianist to do much about it himself. (But see the article by Sol Babitz in *The Musical Quarterly* for October, 1952.) Approximate double-dotting of slower dotted notes is ventured by some (as in the opening of Bach's Partita No. 2 in C minor). But few dare to give a quasi-triple, trochaic or iambic, lilt to slower pairs of eighth-notes. Perhaps our purist attitudes of today compel us to stop short at this license. Or pianists may well fear they would be charged with faulty rather than expressive rhythm.

The dynamics signs are further aids that must be planned and written in when a Bach *Urtext* edition is used. The nature of the instrument intended could give some historical basis for deciding them. But Bach himself seems not to have wanted to delimit his use of the word "clavier" (to mention the long-time question) except in those few instances where he further specified the harpsichord or organ. Even if the harpsichord alone had been intended, one could not play the modern piano and altogether rule out its capabilities for graduated dynamics. Yet, simplicity is the word again. As we have seen, "terrace dynamics" and broad or brief echo effects were favorite Baroque means of keeping the total structure in view. Based on internal cadences and similar landmarks, a few "terrace" changes are suggested in Ex. 24. Note that fugues tend to be cumulative in force but do not always have to build up in volume to the end.

In any new piece there is one further kind of planning that is best done before the fingering can be worked out and the practicing itself started. That is the planning for the most efficient touch mechanisms in every situation throughout the piece (see pages 51 to 65). If these are left to chance the playing can hardly be other than nondescript. For specific illustrations let us see what situations must be met in our three main examples.

Starting from the beginning of the Bach, the portato dots above the subject, and even the staccato dots at this moderate speed, are typically played by the full arm worked as a one-piece unit. A break at the wrist would only complicate the control. In measure 2 the full arm, as always, initiates the new slur or handful of notes. It often initiates trills and turns, too, especially when they start by repeating a tone as in measure 7. The sixteenth-notes will be played legato by the fingers. After these first few touch situations no essentially different ones occur in this fairly uniform piece.

The problem is more varied and detailed in Mozart. In Ex. 25 the heavy, staccato tones in measures 1 to 2 and 19 to 22 call for the strength and accuracy of the forearm. The full arm can supplement the fingers to supply a slight accent on the dissonant upper starting note of the trill in measures 2, 15, and the like. This note is the climactic point of the little rise and fall suggested by the added signs and inherent in each "feminine incise" (see pages 97 to 98). All slurs, whether in measures 3, 9, 18, 23, or 30, will be initiated, as before, by the full arm, acting as the prime mover and transporter of the hand to each new coverage of notes. (In measures 16 and 17 the dotted slurs indicate what I take to be Mozart's actual intention.) The wrist best suits the crisp staccato generally understood in Classic allegro music on the last note of a slur not followed by a rest, or on independent repeated notes. See measures 3, 27, and 31 for different examples. In measure 3 and similar places the hand has to draw back at the wrist to play the staccato note that ends the slur, then rebound thereafter to repeat this note (as explained on pages 61 to 62). Arm rotation can be used to play the broken octaves starting in measure 9, although fingers alone can control them at least as well. In the upper staff of these measures a finger legato is needed that will be supple enough to permit lateral stretches. The notes in the bass staff from measure 13 are played by the hand rebounding from the wrist until measures 17 and 18, where the full arm best plays such separate, deliberate notes. The tied and slurred chord group that crosses the barline between measures 13 and 14 is really a two-note masculine incise, as suggested by the dotted slur and the diminish sign that are added. To avoid giving a separate impulse to the chord of release (and so making a common fault in technique and musicianship) one must play both chords as though his arm were passing six o'clock in a steady clock-wise arc. The masculine group across the barline from measure 31 to 32 and elsewhere can be played in one follow-through motion, too. The best advice for portato repeated notes as in measure 34 is to stay on the key, use the full arm from the shoulder with no break at any other joint, and connect the tones as much as possible.

In the Chopin Prelude, Ex. 26, the full arm again initiates each slur and supplements the fingers to provide any group accents within the runs. The separate eighth-note chords are all played by the forearm except for the right hand's share during a held note, as in measure 1, where the force will have to come from the shoulder. For better tone control the last, longer two chords can be started with fingers on the keys and played by the full arms, pushing up and forward and permitting a slight give at the wrists. The fast octaves in measures 13 and 14 can be played as a series of diminishing wrist rebounds or reverberations initiated by one full-arm impulse. The fast staccatos in measure 18 are best played by strongly articulated finger action (page 59).

The fundamental problem of finding and writing down a good fingering has been saved for the last topic in this section on "laying the groundwork." The reason is that the fingering will be determined in part by the decisions on styles and interpretation. General principles were offered on pages 38 to 44 and 74 to 81. Specific applications are illustrated or cited here. Many of them will appear unconventional, to say the least, to those who have not discovered the values of rapid arm shifts from handful to handful of notes, or the freer use of the thumb on black keys. But remember: Anything is fair in love, war, and piano playing!

The fingering should be worked out in detail by taking each hand alone, a section at a time. However, the interrelation of the hands must be watched constantly. If one hand straddles the other, as in measure 6 of Ex. 24 and in much of Ravel's *Ondine*, or crosses the other as in Scarlatti's familiar Sonata in A major (L. 345 or K. 113), then which hand goes over or under and what fingers will be least in the way must be considered. If the two hands are playing a parallel passage like that in Ex. 26, measures 3 to 5, 9 to 13, or 18 then much confusion is saved by making the thumb or other shifts at the same time. Strength and speed in runs can be increased by dividing the run between the hands, which is a possibility suggested in measure 17 of Ex. 26. However, smoothness would certainly be sacrificed in more delicate passages like that in Beethoven's Sonata in E-flat major, op. 31, no. 3, first movement, measures 53 to 57 (though dividing works well in measures 72 to 75). When the hands share notes on the same staff a thin wavy line can be used to show the distribution that is decided (Ex. 24, measures 21 to 26).

A good way to begin fingering is to take one handful or coverage of notes at a time, *regardless of what fingers land on which black or white keys*. This modern approach, already mentioned several times, is one basis for today's "position technique" (page 81) and for the phenomenal virtuosity displayed by some of today's foremost pianists (including some very agile jazz pianists). To find the first handful simply hold down each successive note until all the fingers are used up. Within the limits of the technique, the starting finger should be the one that permits the largest number of coming notes to be covered while at least one finger serves as a pivot. See Ex. 25, measures 2 to 3 in the right hand and 3 to 4, or 24, in the left. Two clusters underlie the choice of fingering in the slurred group of measures 11 to 13. Bridging over rests, slurs, staccatos, or separate arm attacks need make little difference in the application of this principle, nor even small technical disadvantages. See Ex. 25, measures 17 to 18. The idea is to achieve the maximum simplicity and logic, with the fewest shifts of position (especially shifts by passing the thumb under). Usually simplicity and technical convenience go together. But if there must be a choice, as in a sequence where one of the recurring figures seems to play easier with a different fingering (page 79), then mental ease generally outweighs physical ease as an aid to secure, controlled performance. We have seen that a complicated fingering imperils memorizing. Anxiety in this respect can have a much more paralyzing effect on the

Ex. 26

technique than an awkward stretch or a taxing use of a weaker finger.

Often it is desirable or necessary to cover more than five notes in the handful. If there are six notes one finger can do double duty, usually the thumb. If there are seven, two fingers can play twice or the thumb can do triple duty. This extra duty can be managed in several ways. In Ex. 24, measure 19, the thumb interpolates in a five-finger progression to give a "sixth finger" without disturbing the third finger pivot on A that lasts into measure 22. In Ex. 26, measure 10, the slide on both the thumb in the left hand and the fifth finger in the right hand permits six notes to be covered and thus avoids an extra thumb-under shift. In Ex. 25, measure 23, the second finger actually transfers from G to A-flat in the Alberti bass so that the five tones can be covered by four fingers, saving the fifth finger for the next measure. Working backward from a point at which the fingering is fairly certain was mentioned as a good way to find some of these less obvious possibilities (page 77). In Ex. 24, by starting back from the third and fifth fingers on which measures 19 to 22 are anchored, the fingering for the handful of seven different pitches in measure 18 can be derived.

Passing the thumb under is done too often, not only within groups of notes better taken in one handful, but as if it were the sole means of shifting to a new handful. More resourcefulness is needed, especially in double notes, to exploit the values of crossing under or over another finger; of sliding, even from a white to a black key on occasion; or of simply using the same finger twice. Many times in Bach one of these three devices comes to the rescue when the fingering seems to have reached a dead end.

In Ex. 24, measures 6 to 7, the skip from fifth finger to thumb makes a simple and strong approach to the repeated C that starts the trill. Meanwhile the right-hand fifth finger can play twice, assuming the slurs are used as suggested. In measures 46 to 47, by passing the second finger over the fifth, one shift of position is avoided. In measure 11 the alternative fingering calls for a cross under or a slide. The slide is convenient in measure 52. The unconventional fingering in measures 54 and 55 stems from the pivot of the third finger on B-flat and requires that the thumb pass *over* the fourth finger to the black key, a very effective technique once its strangeness is conquered. Similar is the crossing over of the third finger in Ex. 25, measure 2. In Ex. 24, measures 30 to 33, the handfuls can be preserved and much fuss avoided by simply transferring the thumb and second finger as marked. The legato will suffer no more this way than it does in the more complex solutions usually given. At higher speeds the transfer would hardly be heard (except as clean articulation), any more than the single frames of a movie film are distinguished separately. An odd but successful instance is the use of the third finger on both A-flat and C in the main theme of the finale in Beethoven's Sonata "Appassionata," measure 20.

The fourth finger is generally used, and sometimes the third, on black octaves. But these fingers are an advantage on white octaves only when the stretch permits. Sample uses that give a sense of coverage are suggested in Ex. 26, measure 16. The problem arises often, for example, in the left hand bass of the main theme in Brahms' *Rhapsody* in E-flat major, op. 119, no. 4; or in Chopin's "Butterfly" Etude, where a large right hand can start to good advantage with the third finger on top, then 4, 5, 4, 5, 4, and then the same pattern three notes lower. Legato chord connections, as in measures 13 to 14 of Ex. 25, must be based on total coverage, too, with any repeating finger(s) lifted in advance (the thumb in this instance), as explained on page 60. Connecting the top notes is most important, of course. Changing fingers on a repeated note is disadvantageous to control except in two circumstances. Speed may compel the change, as on the two F's over the barline between measures 14 and 15 of Ex. 25. And the repeated note itself provides an ideal pivot on which to change hand positions, as in measure 1 of Ex. 26. Conversely, in measure 13, by repeating the second finger in the right hand, one has the advantage of securing the leap to the chord. In most editions of Beethoven's Sonata in E-flat major, op. 31, no. 3, a change of fingers is prescribed for the repeated notes in the galloping finale, beginning at measure 12. This change is more than wasteful, since the repeated notes occur in different slurs played by separate attacks of the full arm.

In the innumerable sequences or other recurring figures throughout piano literature, both technical and mental advantages were claimed when each recurrence could be fingered as one handful, with one and the same fingering pattern. See Ex. 25, measures 21 to 22, right hand, and Ex. 24, measures 68 to 69, both hands. The advantages are made still greater by the recurrence of the figure at the same place in the measure, as usually happens. A longer example is the rotary figure after the middle of Rachmaninoff's *Humoresque* (which can be fingered 1, 5, 4, 2 in *every* instance). Such a figure can be set in motion each time by some appropriate thrust of the full arm from the shoulder. When the pianist is enterprising enough to find and get used to these patterns, the results are strength for group accents as desired and that peace of mind gained by not having to watch for a change in some one of the patterns. Ordinarily, one thinks of starting the pattern with an outer finger (thumb or fifth) so that the hand can receive the arm impulse better by rolling with it slightly to either side. Yet the pulsating figure that descends at the start of Chopin's "Revolutionary" Etude is usually and strongly played with arm drops on the second finger to accent the beat.

STEPS 4 TO 6: LEARNING THE NOTES

The next three steps, in this second phase of learning, need only to be summarized briefly here, since there is but little way to illustrate them beyond the discussions in previous chapters and short of actual practice.

Fixing the habits and co-ordinations. If there is ever a time when slow, cautious practice is needed, or when the motto "Hesitate rather than err" applies, it is when the new habits are getting started. Then a few right playings are more than repaid by rapid progress, and a few wrong ones by slow progress plus the work that must be undone before it can be redone. All this was emphasized on pages 104 to 108 and elsewhere. So were the facts that it is better to go right through the piece at this stage as many times as the schedule permits, not stopping to go back or do small-section practice; and that all aspects of the playing must begin at once and grow together, including the correct touches.

The exception to this last is pedaling, which must not be added until the legato, tone balance, and other touch habits can be formed and observed critically, much as violin vibrato is best delayed until the bowing and intonation are worked out. If necessary, the counting aloud may be prepared by clapping the more intricate rhythms in advance (pages 85 to 86). And each hand may be played alone at first to reduce the number of things to keep in mind. Then, when the hands are first combined, special care must be taken. For them to co-ordinate the various conflicting lines, rhythms, or touches such as occur in Exs. 24 and 25 presents a pat-your-head-and-rub-your-tummy problem. Besides, a particular touch that proves to be the only possibility at a fast speed may seem awkward at the slow-practice tempo—for instance, the use of the wrist to play the octaves in Ex. 26, measures 13 and 14. It is too bad such places cannot be played fast from the start. But they cannot, and they must be practiced as they will be played. If the student cannot manage to look before he leaps into mistakes, he might try stopping *before each note* to ask these questions: What is the note? Is it changed by an accidental? Which hand and finger play it? What count, if any, does it fall on? In what style is it played? What touch mechanism is used? This method may seem far removed from the musical goal but it gets the point across.

Counting with the metronome at a slow tempo. (See pages

82 to 83.) This is the first of the steps that will take the piece off one level and "boost" it up to the next. Even at a slow tempo the notes that were but isolated sounds before will now begin to be heard in larger musical relationships, whether of melody, rhythm, harmony, or the total structure. The new step should begin as soon as the conscious note reading (if not peering) ends and the habits have clearly become habits, strong enough to withstand an error now and then. If even the slow tempo seems too fast, the beat may be subdivided at first so that the metronome comes on the "ands" as well (see page 83).

Memorizing. Memorizing slows the piece down at first but soon proves to give it another big boost. On pages 110 to 116 the types and general methods of memorizing were discussed. Do not forget to keep the score out of sight while playing, from now on. Among patterns and relationships to look for, sequences are outstanding aids, especially when the figure, meter, and fingering tally, as discussed earlier. When the entire piece can be recalled, however haltingly, the most effective way to clinch the memory is to start counting at a slow tempo with the metronome again.

STEPS 7 TO 9: PLAYING THE MUSIC

Counting with the metronome up to tempo. Here is still another boost for the piece. It applies chiefly to pieces that are fast or otherwise difficult for the learner. The effort to play up to tempo may mean some splashing and struggling on the way. But that is what the higher speed takes, there is not likely to be any other way, and the correct habits should now be beyond easy destruction. Often, playing the successive handfuls as simultaneous clusters helps to pull up the tempo (page 47). For the most efficient touches, without waste motion, and for the ease and security that come with reserve power, the metronome should occasionally be set 5 to 10 per cent higher than needed. But slow practice must be resumed at regular intervals in the practice, too, if the habits are not to start breaking down. (See pages 44 and 108 to 109.)

Polishing in small-section practice. The efforts to bring the piece up to tempo will bring those hardest spots to the fore that did not fall into line during any of the earlier steps. Now is the best time to conquer them, practicing in small sections where necessary. The method recommended more than once here is to create exercises out of these actual situations. Besides the procedures mentioned on pages 45 to 47, a method of converting figures or handfuls into double-note exercises may now be described. This last procedure quickly reveals the weakness in a figure; or in one's technique, for that matter, since it gets at the real criterion, which is finger independence and co-ordination, not mere noise and uncontrolled speed. It usually corrects the weakness, too, by developing both the feel and best angle of the hand for the cluster and the weak co-ordination in question.

The double notes are found by taking each possible combination of notes within a figure of three, four, or five *different pitches* (which may mean many more notes). In a sense, one permutes the figure. In Ex. 24, if the three pitches used in the trill and suffix in measures 7 to 8 do not play smoothly the bottom two can be played as one double note and alternated with the top one, tremolo fashion; or the top two with the bottom one, or the outer two with the inner one. These pairings can be represented by the suggested fingering: $\frac{2}{3}$ vs. 1, $\frac{1}{2}$ vs. 3, and $\frac{1}{3}$ vs. 2. In all exercises of this sort legato, exaggerated finger action must be used, with no arm jogging (pages 54 to 56), and the alternation must be in triplet meter so that each side gets the strengthening benefits of the accent. Timesavers and devotees of limbering exercises might well let the other hand "come along for the ride," too. The four-pitch group in the trill from measures 2 to 3 in Ex. 25 can be practiced: $\frac{3}{2}$ vs. $\frac{5}{4}$, $\frac{4}{2}$ vs. $\frac{5}{3}$, and $\frac{5}{2}$ vs. $\frac{4}{3}$. And in Ex. 26, measure 11, the five-pitch group on the last beat can be practiced (to take just the right hand): $\frac{3}{2}$ vs. $\frac{5}{4}$, $\frac{4}{2}{\scriptstyle 1}$ vs. $\frac{5}{3}{\scriptstyle 1}$ vs. $\frac{5}{2}{\scriptstyle 1}$ vs. $\frac{4}{3}{\scriptstyle 1}$ vs. $\frac{4}{3}{\scriptstyle 1}$ vs. $\frac{5}{2}{\scriptstyle 1}$ vs. $\frac{4}{2}$, $\frac{5}{4}{\scriptstyle 1}$ vs. $\frac{3}{2}{\scriptstyle 2}$ vs. $\frac{4}{3}{\scriptstyle 1}$ vs. $\frac{5}{1}{\scriptstyle 2}$ vs. $\frac{4}{4}{\scriptstyle 2}$ vs. $\frac{3}{1}$, and $\frac{5}{4}{\scriptstyle 3}$ vs. $\frac{2}{1}$! But if this much detail almost kills the patient in order to effect the cure, he can try the simpler combination of five pitches: $\frac{3}{1} - \frac{4}{2} - \frac{5}{3} - \frac{4}{2}$, and so on.

If no such remedy helps, perhaps a different fingering, redistribution between the hands, or touch mechanism can be tried. Or perhaps the passage is a climactic one where the pianist can make a virtue out of his difficulties by broadening the tempo a bit (as at the final canon and subject entry in Franck's *Prelude, Choral, and Fugue*). Or, assuming the rest of the piece goes well enough, it may even be necessary to thin out or simplify the notes themselves a bit, on the theory that the total effect is more important than the details. This last secret of the trade is a musical sacrilege, to be sure, but one that seems to be the rule rather than the exception in some pieces (for example, the opening of Ravel's *Ondine*).

Other polishing is in order at this point, too. The touches must be re-examined to see if they are affording the most economical and athletically graceful solution to each situation—the best follow-through, swing, elasticity, "dog-paddle" alternation of the hands, or other co-ordination *as these may help to further the music's meaning* (pages 51 to 65). The joints must not break unnecessarily. (Recall the rubber-handled hoe.) Is the staccato crisp enough for its context? Is the legato faulty because of failure to hold the arm still, stay on the keys, cover the handfuls, stretch laterally, pedal clearly, or group the tones sufficiently?

The pedaling itself needs special attention now. (See pages 69 to 71.) Polyphony at most permits only careful "flutter" pedaling except where there are chords to enrich, as at cadences. A melodic line must be heard as a line. Even when it outlines chords, as does the subject of Bach's two-part Invention in A minor, it must not be reduced to a diffuse chordal mass by the pedal. Thus, in Chopin's Prelude in D-flat major the pedal is best delayed at the start until at least the second if not the third melody note is reached, the more so in a descending chord outline because the highest tone would continue to predominate. Pedaling through rests is often questionable. For example, notwithstanding contradictory pedal markings, Chopin seems to have meant what he wrote in the Scherzo in B-flat minor, measure 5, when he put a staccato under the B-flat and two quarter rests after it. This effect of a startled gasp before the crash can be very dramatic.

While listening critically to the pedaling the student must *hear* the melody tone and the total sonority he is producing (pages 65 to 69). Is the balance good, with not too much bass, enough melody to "sing," yet no missing tones in the harmony? Does each melody tone get about equal emphasis, with no loss of importance because it is on a weak beat, short in duration, or the bottom of a leap? A good exercise for control of key descent (page 68) and balance is the playing of one chord twenty times by the full arm as one unit, from soft to loud and back to soft. The problem is to make a steady rise and fall, and to project any one tone constantly in the same proportion. Whatever the touch, it is always harder to play soft than loud. Getting closer to the keys and lowering the wrist often help, as they do, for example, in a delicate piece like Mendelssohn's Scherzo in E minor.

Interpreting the piece as a whole. This final step is needed in order to see more clearly the forest of which the trees are a part (page 93). Every aspect of interpretation must be reconsidered to see whether it is contributing to the final goal, which might be stated as meaningful projection of the total form—or more simply, as getting the musical message across.

The markings need to be rechecked at this time. Original markings are a free lesson from the composer and certainly the most authoritative lesson of all. How often a student will work hard on a Debussy Prelude without ever thinking to look up the meaning of the very precisely worded French instructions! The prescribed dynamic and tempo levels must be heeded especially, so that the valleys and peaks of the form are in good perspective, from the most relaxed moment to the overall climax (page 103). The same perspective must be sought even throughout the contrasting movements of an extended suite or sonata. Recently, one New York critic, still tired from the previous season, began his review of the first Town Hall recital in the new season, "Well, the young pianists are off again, louder and faster than ever!" Mature artists do not anesthetize their audiences in this way. By giving meaning to everything, they can afford to play much of the time in a quiet "speaking voice" and well under their top speed, making the few real climaxes far more exciting.

Every phrase needs to be re-examined to see if its meaning is clearly understood. Does it go to and from somewhere? Is there a climactic point that is musically convincing (pages 94 to 96)? A useful rule of thumb is the one that says no note should occur twice in the same phrase in the same way.

Occasional rechecks with the metronome keep the prevailing tempo in mind and ward off eccentricities in the performance. Driving music must keep driving. All the while the train is passing all sorts of scenery or going through tunnels the tackety-tack of railroad ties keeps up its steady beat. On the other hand, there must be those breathing spots that can only come after many playings. These occur, of course, at phrase endings, and more so at the broader and broader divisions in the form. They are sometimes equally necessary for endurance (page 123).

To bring all these factors together in one unified, convincing, well-controlled performance takes many complete playings of the piece and a fair amount of time. One must figure on several weeks or more between the day when the piece has first been played up to tempo without hitches from memory to the day of the first public performance. During that time the piece should mature and change from a "new piece" to a piece in the pianist's repertoire.

VI. Il Maestro e lo Scolare

THIS brief, concluding chapter borrows its title from that charming duet by Haydn in which each variation by the teacher is faithfully imitated by the pupil. It deals, in fact, with two interesting questions of teaching methods that have been at the center of numerous books, articles, and discussions in the piano world of recent years. One concerns a new approach to piano study through sight reading, the other a comparison of learning by facts and learning by intuition and imagery. My own inclinations in these matters are made clear enough in this book. But it should become equally clear that no single, final answers are either necessary or possible. Too much depends on the individual background, personality, and educational philosophy of each teacher.

THE SIGHT-READING APPROACH

In a significant little book called *Guided Sight Reading* the late Leonhard Deutsch explained his method of developing pianists from scratch to advanced performers entirely through sight reading. For the details and some real nuggets of teaching wisdom the reader is urged to see this book for himself (listed in Source References). Here the remarks are spent only on the use of the method in the first year or so of study and on what some of us have concluded through our own experiments to be a far more sensible approach than the traditional inductive one.

Traditionally the beginner is introduced to piano playing one item at a time in a logical sequence. "This is a piano. You sit in front of it, so. There are eighty-eight white and black keys. See how the black keys are arranged in twos and threes. Middle C is to the left of the two-black-key group and in front of your nose. Play middle C with this thumb." And so forth! Not so with Mr. Deutsch. In effect, he seats the beginner at the piano, with the first little piece on the rack, puts his finger on the starting note, and tells him, "O.K., begin playing. When the notes go up you go up; when they go down you go down." The "guided" part of the sight reading means mainly that the teacher plays along with the student in a higher octave or at a second piano, thus giving him the idea of the music and the support to keep it going. Explanations are given only as the student needs them to advance in this manner, or as he himself requests them.

Mr. Deutsch's argument, paraphrased here, is that the beginner does not learn inductively, step by step, but reaches at once to reproduce the total result as best he can. A child learns to walk not from gradual training in the use of the fibula and metatarsus, or some such, but by imitating grownups as he struggles right off to get to the cookie held before him.

Six important advantages might be claimed for the sight-reading approach, which goes even further and more directly into piano learning than rote teaching or the various five-finger position systems. First, the immediate, ever-present incentive or goal is music itself. *One learns piano to make enjoyable music.* This is a goal easily lost sight of at any stage of learning, what with so much emphasis on the means to the end—on trick methods, exercises for their own sake, pretty covers, or other inducements mentioned in the previous chapter. Second, *the student experiences success at once.* Neat explanations that seem so necessary and systematic to the initiated simply try the patience of the novice. In fact, they can soon kill his interest because they seem so remote from the goal.

A third advantage is that *all practice is supervised at first,* that practice being the lesson itself (a recommendation that only the parents may not readily understand and accept). When the beginner is a young child, to expect straight, independent practice often seems unreasonable. An ideal schedule, even for the supervised practice, might be one that permits each child to come for, say, three ten-minute lessons a week rather than one half hour. Fourth, the sight-reading approach *permits the learner to discover meanings and relationships for himself.* When he does discover them, they are likely to make more sense than the most logical, careful explanations from an outside source. It is strange what curious gaps those explanations often leave in the student's mind.

Fifth, this approach *favors reading not by single pitches and note values but by contours, groups, and patterns* (in the manner that children are now taught to read words, in spite of recent controversies). The fact may be hard for some to believe, but the line and staff and the note values are learned much more readily in this way and with the details only filled in as the student requests them (if he has not discovered them for himself!). Sixth and last, *the teacher who turns to this newer approach is likely to feel that she herself has won a new lease on her teaching life.* Gone is the struggle to win and hold the interest. The music itself wins the student over and keeps him.

The object in these first years is not perfection but broad keyboard experience in as varied and as much music as possible. (Deutsch himself left a collection of charming folk-song arrangements for this purpose.) It seems strained and optimistic to insist on refinements, such as any special hand position, at a time when gross motor controls are still being learned. The child totters precariously before he himself corrects his form. Public recitals may well be only a barrier in early training (another idea that parents in particular would need to accept). Technique work could be limited to simple exercises that develop a feel for the spacing of the keys and an awareness of the four playing mechanisms (see pages 51 to 52). For the fingers the chromatic scale in the standard fingering and the sequential pattern of the first of the Hanon Daily Exercises can be learned with surprising ease. For the wrist parallel thirds in the two hands, up and down the white keys, answer well. The forearm can do triads in the same manner, while for the full arm the beginner enjoys inventing his own hand-over-hand patterns that repeat at each octave level, "dog-paddle" style. Going from the bottom to the top of the keyboard and back is a good way to define the extent of these exercises. (The littlest tots cannot sit but have to walk to do this.)

My own belief is that Mr. Deutsch's approach is excellent at the beginning (and always as a means of developing sight reading itself), but that it must presently be replaced by something like the inductive one detailed in the previous chapter. In other words, as the student gets more and more into single works that he would actually like to perfect and perform he must change more and more to systematic, stey-by-step learning. But in the realm of elementary training, enterprising and adventuresome teachers may find that the sight-reading approach can revolutionize the traditional teaching methods.

LEARNING BY INTUITION, IMAGERY, OR FACTS?

In recent years, not only Mr. Deutsch but Luigi Bonpensiere, Abby Whitesides, Lilias Mackinnon, and others have written highly stimulating books that argue largely for a more direct approach to the whole musical composition or *Gestalt* as the sum of more than its parts. Whether that approach is through rhythm, mental attitude, or other means the idea is to sense and work for that goal. Objections are voiced against what one author aptly calls "notewise" practice and the self-conscious, studied performance it might produce; and against systematic explanations about what is essentially an art and not a science. Similarly to Mr. Shepherd's thoughtful remarks quoted on pages 65 to 66, these authors feel that concentration on an aural image of the piece will direct the learning subconsciously, more efficiently and musically than any conscious, piecemeal methods of building up to performance level.

These authors themselves have all done very successful teaching. Furthermore, one cannot deny, on the one hand, that their first interest is a thoroughly musical performance and that psychological aids can be very effective (see pages 103 to 104), or, on the other, that academicians can easily miss that extra something that completes the *Gestalt*. For my own part I think of only three reservations to be made—cautions rather than objections—in the interest of less experienced teachers.

First, the momentum of even the fastest running start toward the goal cannot pick up *all* the details along the way. Certain ornaments simply will not solve themselves, certain fingering will not see ahead to what must come out, certain touches will not co-ordinate without very considerable stopping for analysis,

planning, and that notewise practice. Second, there is always the danger that the psychological inducements (the "python-like writhings," "drum-beat," or "beckoning with a handkerchief" that

Bülow and Lebert asked for in Beethoven) will be exaggerated
to the point of causing actual errors of fact and method. Familiar
examples are the strange touches sometimes developed to evoke
differences of timbre (at the same volume) that simply do not
exist (although more remarkable examples could be cited from
vocal instruction!). Third, it is sometimes easier just to state the
facts. As Arnold Schultz wrote about tone (*The Riddle of the
Pianist's Finger,* page 196), "My own objection to the theory of
voluntary control over tone-quality is based less upon the relationship of the moving hammer to the strings and upon photog-
raphy of sound waves (although this evidence seems incontro-
vertible enough) than it is upon the fact that what people desig-
nate as qualitative differences are explicable in simpler and more
satisfactory terms."

But there really ought be no great divide between the extremes
of subjective and objective teaching. The ideal teacher to break
through this divide, I should think, would be the one capable of
fitting the approach to the student. And he would be the one with
the imagination to stimulate the larger view, yet with the solid
grounding by which to avoid leading his students astray into
more or new pianist's problems.

Some Source References
for Enterprising Pianists

S OME students and teachers will want to peer behind the scenes into the evidence for much that they have read here. Others will want further details about musical form, the history of the piano, or other related subjects. Here is a list of representative publications that should prove helpful.

Putnam Aldrich, *Ornamentation in J. S. Bach's Organ Works*. New York: Coleman-Ross Co., Inc., 1950. Clear and brief, with many examples.

Willi Apel, *Masters of the Keyboard; a brief survey of pianoforte music*. Cambridge (Mass.): Harvard University Press, 1947. Includes many complete music examples from about 1500 to the present.

Carl Philipp Emanuel Bach, *Essay on the True Art of Playing Keyboard Instruments*, translated by William J. Mitchell. New York: W. W. Norton & Co., Inc., 1949. The most celebrated treatise of the eighteenth century.

Thurston Dart, *The Interpretation of Music*. New York: Hutchinson's University Library, 1954. Chiefly about editions and performance practices in older music.

Leonhard Deutsch, *Guided Sight-Reading; a new approach to piano study*. New York: Crown Publishers, 1950.

James Friskin and Irwin Freundlich, *Music for the Piano; a handbook of concert and teaching material from 1580 to 1952*. New York: Rinehart & Co., Inc., 1954.

Scott Goldthwaite, *Ornamentation in Music for the Keyboard*. Chicago: Clayton F. Summy Co. (1954). (No. 5 in the Summy Piano Teaching Pamphlet Series.) Brief but very helpful.

R. E. M. Harding, *A History of the Pianoforte to 1851*. Cambridge (England): Cambridge University Press, 1933. Evolution of the instrument itself.

A. H. Howe, *Scientific Piano Tuning and Servicing.* New York: published by the author, 116 Pinehurst Avenue, 1941. Includes useful illustrations.

Alice M. Kern and Helen M. Titus, *The Teacher's Guidebook to Piano Literature; a recommended listing of graded repertoire for elementary, intermediate, and lower advanced students.* Ann Arbor: J. W. Edwards, Inc., 1954. The listing is by centuries, too.

Arthur Loesser, *Men, Women and Pianos; a social history.* New York: Simon and Schuster, 1954. The rich lore of pianos, piano playing, and pianists; highly informative and entertaining.

Matthis Lussy, *Musical Expression,* translated from the French. London: Novello, Ewer, and Co., 1885 and later editions. A fundamental study of intelligent phrasing.

Lilias Mackinnon, *Music by Heart.* Baltimore: The Monumental Publishing Co., 1954. A helpful guide to memorizing.

Howard Murphy and Edwin Stringham, *Creative Harmony and Musicianship, an introduction to the structure of music.* New York: Prentice-Hall, Inc., 1951. Includes many exercises in harmony through elementary composition.

William S. Newman, *Understanding Music; a new introduction to music's elements, styles, and forms—for both the layman and the practitioner.* New York: Harper & Brothers, 1953. A comprehensive background for pianists and others.

Otto R. Ortman, *The Physiological Mechanics of Piano Technique; an experimental study of the nature of muscular action as used in piano playing, and of the effects thereof on the piano key and the piano tone.* New York: E. P. Dutton & Co., Inc., 1929.

Piano Quarterly Newsletter, issued by the Piano Teachers Information Service, 88 Morningside Drive, New York 27, N. Y. An important periodical designed to keep teachers and students up to date on publications and books.

Arnold Schultz, *The Riddle of the Pianist's Finger; and its relationship to a touch scheme.* New York: Carl Fischer, Inc., 1949. A keen analysis of the physiology of piano technique and a critique of other approaches.

Carl Seashore, *Psychology of Music.* New York: McGraw-Hill Book Co., Inc., 1938. Concerns learning and the musician's capabilities.

Index

165